Humor in Advertising

Humor in Advertising

...AND HOW TO MAKE IT PAY

Don Herold

McGRAW-HILL BOOK COMPANY, INC.

New York   Toronto   London

HUMOR IN ADVERTISING

Preface

*Life has more resources
than our reason, and sometimes,
in addition, it has a smile.*
—CLAUDE ANET

A book preface and an after-dinner speech are much alike, except that one comes before and the other after.

I've always thought that banquet tables should have lower berths for the customers during the speeches, but I can think of no device to help preface readers.

Nearly all ceremonies are boresome to me. The President of the United States must get so bored with delivering the same platitudes at the ceremonies which constitute the greater part of his term in office, that he may actually be relieved when a new national crisis arises to call on his higher faculties.

The purpose of this book is expressed in its title, and will be obvious to anybody who reads the first few pages and flips through the rest of them.

To sum it up in advance, however, it is a plea for less boresome ceremony in advertising and for more fun for the creator of advertising and for the reader, and, as a consequence, more profit for the advertiser who pays the bill.

This does not mean hilarity or slapstick or strained cleverness, but just a little letting down of corporate pomposity, and abstinence from unbelievable claims and absurd glorification of merely mundane products. (Even a Cadillac is merely a Cadillac, and heaven knows a detergent is not a thing divine.)

The book is full of examples of good uses of good humor, mostly of the mild type, with a few examples of unhappily inept use of humor thrown in for good measure.

If some of the former are mine, maybe they help point in the direction of what I mean by "humor in advertising."

Don Herold

OTHER BOOKS BY DON HEROLD

So Human
Bigger and Better
There Ought to Be a Law
Strange Bedfellows
Doing Europe and Vice Versa
Love That Golf
Advertising Typographers Association Handbook
The Happy Hypochondriac

Contents

Humor in Advertising

Never be comic in your advertisements. If you are facetious about your product it is fatal. If, on the other hand, you are really humorous, you will put a value on the advertisement that cannot be obtained by any other means.
—FOUGASSE (KENNETH BIRD)

By humor in advertising, I don't mean jokes.

I don't mean gags.

I don't mean gimmicks.

Maybe I don't even mean humor.

I am shy of the word "humor." It has a different meaning for almost everybody.

Before I got seriously (there I go!) into advertising, I once belonged to an organization known as the American Press Humorists. I tried to get them to change their name, on the grounds that no group of real humorists would call themselves humorists.

Later I belonged to a more profound assembly of madmen, a Tuesday luncheon club in Hollywood known as the West Side Asthma and Riding Club. It had been named by S. J. Perelman and was presided over by Groucho Marx.

Perhaps it would be apropos if I interrupted myself right here with a quotation from myself in a piece I wrote some years ago in some magazine on the subject of humor:

Humor is a funny thing.

What is humor, anyway? It is a sort of differential gear which enables us to keep both wheels on the ground and run along without jolts in spite of the variation between the way things ought to be and the way they are. God knew that people would bump into each other and stumble over things, so He saw it would be necessary to put a little "give" in human nature. Humor is the "give." If folks were entirely brittle, the entire human race would be cracked into smithereens in a few months. Someone once said: "God could not be everywhere, so He made mothers." It is equally true that for the same reason (that He could not be everywhere to explain things) He made funny bones.

Humor, in short, provides amiable acceptance. Isn't this the number one thing we are seeking in advertising? Humor establishes an atmosphere of give or give-in, instead of belligerent defense.

By humor in advertising, I mean a quiet and sensible and legitimate use of amusing copy and/ or cartoons, or perhaps amusing illustrations or photographs, to do a job of merchandising—first by attracting attention in a *relevant* way, then by imparting pleasant information and making a soft sell, all in a mixed atmosphere of relaxation and integrity.

People are not fools. They know well enough that the complete salvation of the human race does not depend on the universal use of somebody's detergent or underarm deodorant. Merchandise is just not that important.

"No one gets as glad as that over anything in this world," says Gilbert Seldes.

To some extent, perhaps the tide is turning.

Says *Printers' Ink:* "For one thing, many ad men are becoming increasingly weary of the fast, fast, fast sell and are afraid the public is wearier yet."

So many advertisers are so long-faced in deliverance of their "message" that it is totally ingratiating when one of them admits his product is not a thing divine.

"We absolutely detest perfection in other human beings. When your product openly confesses that it falls a little short of perfection it gains a more likeable, believable image," says *Printers' Ink* further.

I like Texaco's slogan for its Sky Chief gasoline: "The nearest thing yet to a perfect gasoline." *That* is almost humor.

Benjamin Franklin put it this way:

The best way to convince another is to state your case moderately and accurately. Then scratch your head or shake it a little and say it is the way it seems to you, but that of course you may be mistaken about it. . . . The best way to win with even the most difficult souls is never to be completely sure of yourself. And show it.

Maybe by humor I mean, among other things, moderation.

" 'Suaviter in modo, fortiter in re,' is the advice of Aquaviva, which, in United States, is to say, 'If your case is good, there is no need to yell,' " wrote Uncle Dudley.

"Humor is actual truth" said no less a scholar than Red Skelton.

The most delightful experience I, personally, ever had in advertising concerns the response made by a little old lady who came into the office of one of a number of savings and loan associations for whom I prepare weekly ads. She laid down $10,000 in savings at the teller's window, and upon being asked how she had happened to come to this particular bank, replied: "I have been reading your weekly cartoon ads, and they seemed so honest that I felt this would be a good safe place for my money."

Not too many years ago, *Time* magazine, in an article entitled "The Sophisticated Sell," said: "Instead of bludgeoning the customer with razzle-dazzle headlines and ranting copy, admen today are appealing to him with quiet humor, soft talk and attractive art. . . . More and more advertisers are taking the position that an ounce of charm can be worth a pound of pressure."

Well, let's say *some* advertisers are.

I like humor quiet and I do know that the first earmark of a good, humorous advertisement is sincerity. Then, the more fun the better. Because fun says: "Step up a little closer, ladies and gentlemen"

Sincerity can cover such a multitude of sins or shortcomings. I find that Judy Garland's voice *does* get a little fuzzy around the edges, but I always love to hear her. I've always wondered why, until I read a quotation from her as follows: "I really mean every word of every song I sing, no matter how many times I've sung it before."

The late great actor, William Gillette, was thinking of the same thing when, in explaining his technique, he said he always strove to give the illusion of "doing the thing for the first time," not on the stage, but in real life, as if it were actually happening, with hems and haws and hesitations.

In a speech at a convention of the Advertising Federation of America, John P. Cunningham, chairman of Cunningham & Walsh, Inc., elaborated on this theme by taking as his text a 125-year-old advertisement for a straw bonnet, which ended with these words:

This advertiser, by the good quality of his materials and moderate prices, hopes to merit a share of the public patronage, and to retain it by a strict and steady attention to business.

The very restraint of this announcement gives it humor.

Continued Mr. Cunningham: "Compare that simple, earnest bonnet advertisement with some of those gorgeous, graphic effusions used to sell bonnets now."

Mr. Cunningham and I are backed up by a fine piece by James D. Woolf in *Advertising Age*, from which I quote the following:

According to the measurements of Dr. Starch and other slide-rulers, the readership ratings of printed advertising, taken by and large, are nothing to cheer about.

There are a number of reasons for the consumer's failure to gobble up eagerly even the costly prose of our allegedly talented pitchmen. The dominant reason, which embraces all the others, is that much copy is a *perfectly frightful bore*.

The fact is, that the secret of capturing reader interest is to be found in the sheer artistry of the copywriter. Consider, for example, the problem of selling pears by mail. If the copywriter were to pattern his approach after the conventional style of so much current advertising, his headlines would run along this line: "*Revolutionary! The Most Amazing Pears This Side of Heaven!*"

But that isn't the way G. Lynn Sumner did it for Harry and David Rosenberg, who operate orchards in Medford, Oregon. His first magazine advertisement for Royal Riviera pears—"*Imagine Harry and Me advertising our PEARS in Fortune!*"—was tremendously successful and won an Annual Advertising Awards certificate as the best advertisement in the year it appeared.

Now, that may not be a scream, but it fits my idea of humor in advertising.

Humor by Committee? NO!

One thing I know and that is that humor cannot be produced by a committee.

I look at many advertisements which seem banal or inarticulate or overproduced and I can imagine the talk that went on about them "in conference." The agency presented them to the client with a fine-sounding explanation, but the ads don't say what the explanation said they'd say.

Humor is something of a divine spark, and sparks usually happen to individuals, not to committees. Can you imagine Beethoven calling a committee meeting to write his Fifth Symphony or can you even imagine Irving Berlin calling in his board of directors to help him compose "White Christmas"?

When Claude Hopkins thought of "In the gentle hands of shepherds they found the clue to GENTLE SHAVING" for Williams Shaving Cream, he probably did it in his shower and not in a conference. He may, of course, have tested it in Des Moines before he turned it loose on all America.

Incidentally, I believe that an office is the worst place on earth in which to think of anything. For years I used to leave my office and take a pad and pencil across the street to the waiting room of Grand Central Station when I had any creative work to do. Then I almost quit going to the office altogether, and worked at home. I still have an office but I spent only two days there last year, and only ten days the year before. The help say I bother them when I come in, and God knows they bother me.

Though "My Fair Lady" was probably given an out-of-town tryout before it was brought into New York, I'm sure George Bernard Shaw didn't even ask Mrs. Shaw what she thought of "Pygmalion" (on which "My Fair Lady" was based).

Countless good campaigns are murdered in committee by that "sound thinker," present in almost every conference, who tries to wet down all playful impulses. He has stayed on the company payroll for decades because he has a consistently and automatically cautious and negative attitude. He has all his associates scared with his sound, negative thinking. It's the easiest role an unimaginative job holder can grab for himself in an organization. I've seen him everywhere I go, and I abhor the reverence he usually commands.

But should all this seem to indicate that all that is needed to achieve effective humor in advertising is total abandon, I can cite many examples to prove that there isn't anything as heavy as the light touch in advertising when it is done the wrong way. The technique is that of delicate surgery—like operating on a thyroid gland which is only a quarter of an inch away from the jugular vein, where even the slightest slip can be fatal to the patient.

You can see the casualties from inexpert use of humor in every issue of almost any magazine, and in many television commercials. Results are often as disastrous as the gaiety of a drunk from Kokomo trying to live it up on a dance floor in New York with a clumsy 1940 one-step. Or of the legendary country club cut-up who dons a lampshade as a woman's hat.

"You Little Money Maker!"

Some magazines unintentionally inspire silliness in advertisers. *The New Yorker*, for instance, often evokes advertising copywriting which turns out to be sickeningly cute and coy in an embarrassing way, or to produce elephantine antics, completely devoid of agility.

One campaign greatly revered by the advertising fraternity has been that of the Hathaway shirt man with the eye patch, but I happen to think the eye patch is at least irrelevant. I would say this is a good way to sell *eye patches,* not shirts.

I know, of course, I will be told that this gimmick has sold trainloads of shirts.

Pardon me, but right here I want to take a stand against the supposedly unanswerable argument, "It sells merchandise." I feel in my heart that the profession of advertising has an obligation above and beyond the call of merchandising. I will belabor this point further later in this book.

And when I am told anything "sells merchandise" I can always counter with, "A better campaign might have sold twice as much." (It would be hard to prove me wrong.)

I am discouraged by the number of imitatively crazy concepts that the eye patch has produced in the hands of lesser talents.

In his book, *Reality in Advertising* (with which I otherwise enjoyably disagree), Rosser Reeves laments this plague of silliness in advertising.

Thus the originality ads begin their endless cycles. One eye-patch (following the bold and correct lead of a David Ogilvy) breeds a succession of mere eye-patches. One beard, on a Commander Whitehead, becomes a thousand useless beards. Men sit on horses backwards; they sip martinis against Sahara sand dunes; they wear evening clothes down into the Caribbean surf; they play white pianos on mountain tops.

As for Commander Whitehead (another Ogilvy account), I am repelled, because I have the personal, perhaps hypochondriacal conviction that all whiskers are germ catchers and should have gone out with Pasteur.

(However, I can forgive Mr. Ogilvy's agency almost anything, because it is responsible for what I regard as perhaps the greatest single line in advertising—in a Rolls-Royce ad: "At 60 m.p.h. the loudest noise comes from the electric clock.")

Another instance of what I, personally, feel is an inappropriate use of humor in advertising is that of General Electric's employment of another partially blind man, Mr. McGoo, in selling electric light bulbs. Here again, I don't care how many kudos this campaign has won or how many light bulbs it has sold. I don't even respond to the logic, "If he, being two-thirds blind, thinks General Electric bulbs produce good illumination, how good they must really be for those of us with normal vision!"

Browne Vintners Company was wise to drop its white horse series—man in yachting costume sitting on a white horse. They were probably led into this by the eye-patch man, but no doubt soon found that there's only a limited market for White Horse Scotch among yachtsmen sitting on white horses.

Lest I seem to be dwelling on the negative at this point, let me call your attention to the fact that I have filled this book largely with examples of real humor in advertising, delightfully used.

"God help you, Hagley, if this ad isn't a success!"

"Far out" advertising was bitingly commented on by *Playboy* in the above cartoon by cartoonist Claude. (FROM *Playboy: Copyright* © *1958, by HMH Publishing Co., Inc.*)

Starting with the eye-patch imitators, Mr. Reeves wades into practically all creative people in advertising.

He calls "originality" the most dangerous word in advertising. "Here, misty, distant, and infinitely desirable, is the copywriter's Holy Grail."

As if dullness, unimaginativeness, soporific sameness, boresomeness and boorishness were qualities with which to win attention, win friends, win sales!

Only the most naïve copywriter (and there are plenty of them) strives for fine writing, unique literary style, "clever conceits." All of the good ones have read Ruskin's comments on style:

For I have had what, in many respects, I boldly call the misfortune, to set my words sometimes prettily together; not without a foolish vanity in the poor knack that I had of doing so; until I was heavily punished for this pride, by finding that many people thought of the words only, and cared nothing for their meaning. Happily, therefore, the power of using such pleasant language—if indeed it ever were mine—is passing away from me, and whatever I am now able to say at all, I find myself forced to say with great plainness.

Rosser Reeves pictures copywriters as a group of dreamy, frustrated literary people who want to have fun with words regardless of what it does to their sponsor's sales.

"Great copywriting, in its way, is not unlike engineering," he writes. "No one will deny that the catenary curve of a bridge is a lovely and sweeping thing. However, the bridge is built for a purpose other than art."

Only a novice at advertising copywriting forgets that a bridge is to get people, cars, trains, and cargoes of merchandise across bodies of water, swamps, or gullies.

I always cringe when I sense that an ad, a campaign, or a television commercial series is being consciously written down to some Neanderthal dimwit—the typical "consumer" many advertisers envision as their target.

"The consumer is not a moron. She is your wife," says David Ogilvy:

An advertiser who deliberately plays dumb for an imaginary twelve-year-old audience is definitely alienating a huge portion of the big American public, which has, I believe, a much greater amount of innate good taste and common sense and sense of the phony (and sense of humor) than we are apt to give it credit for.

Says a Leo Burnett house ad: "It is one of the paradoxes of business that to reach masses you must also reach classes. This is illustrated in show business where the largest audiences are drawn not by performers appealing to lowbrows, but by those appealing to *high and* low."

There may be more of the low, but they come in even greater numbers if they are led by the high. Shakespeare knew you had to get them all, and it was probably the intellectuals who were responsible for his full houses. He had plenty of gore for the pit, but he had glory for the highbrows, so he has had big box offices for generations.

What I fear now is panic flight by the public from the bang-bang repetition of basically dull or even vulgar messages that the wham school is giving the public. The vulgarities of unhumorous printed advertising are less blatant than those of television but they are there, and they too help destroy the power of advertising. Every ridiculous performance in advertising and every attempt to perpetrate the unbelievable is a blow to the profession.

I string along with such evangelists as Ken Baynes, editor of *Graphis* in Zurich: "Advertising has to change from being the dull sledge hammer it is into a genuine popular art that will mean something to the people who see it—something they will remember and talk over, that will enrich their lives and enlarge their experience."

For soap-fishermen

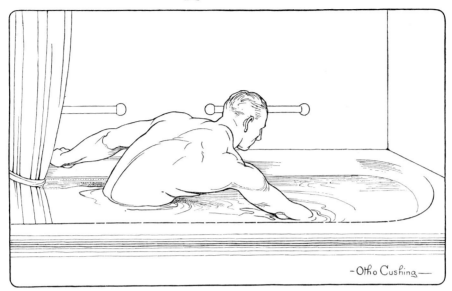

—Otho Cushing—

We sometimes still hear of a man who tries to bathe with a soap that has all the diving properties of a ship's anchor.

The fact is, sinker-soaps went out of fashion for the bath with tin tubs and the one-horse shay.

The Ivory non-sink principle is simple and incontestible. Therefore it is both modern and permanent. Is it desirable that your bath soap should conceal itself, like a furtive trout, in some dark corner of the tub-bottom? No. Very well, that is why Ivory Soap floats.

Ivoryless men are handicapped in other ways, too. For instance, they cannot yet have learned the truth about real lather. Ivory lather differs from most lather as a fleecy summer cloud from a November fog.

To produce a real lather you don't need to do the daily dozen with a cake of Ivory. The effort expended by the Ivoryless bather to manufacture his thin, mucilaginous film would, if he were using Ivory, envelop his form to the point of complete modesty. And Ivory lather disappears in the rinse like a ghost when the lights are turned on.

We propose, gentlemen, an Ivory bath daily for cleanliness and refreshment.

PROCTER & GAMBLE

IVORY SOAP

99 $^{44}/_{100}$ % PURE   IT FLOATS

FOR the 100 or more square inches of exposed skin on your face and hands, we recommend Guest Ivory. It is new. It fits all hands and protects all complexions. Five cents.

From way back in 1924 comes this example of fine, quiet, expert humor in advertising. This is all the more unusual when you consider how rapidly styles in humor change. Consider the dated humor of Josh Billings, Artemus Ward, Mr. Dooley, and even to some extent, that of some of Mark Twain.

I am sure Procter & Gamble wrote the "99 44/100% pure" slogan with tongue in cheek; it is so precise that it is obviously impossible, and therefore funny. It caught on so well that it soon became a common phrase in the American language. This ad has not only humor, but the chaste Otho Cushing outline drawing and the uncluttered typography suggest cleanliness. —(AGENCY: *The Blackman Company*)

"Oh Lord! A blowout, no raincoat and five miles to the nearest town. Why didn't I have sense enough to put on Kelly-Springfields all around!"

An aristocratic ad of 1920 which would take prizes today for good humor, good art (by L. Fellows) and suggestion of quality. Its simple, excellent drawing gives it smash display, and its restraint suggests class certainly not conveyed by most of today's studhorse tire advertising.

*"Thank goodness I have Kelly-Springfield tires on the car.
At least there won't be any trouble from that source."*

Another of the smart L. Fellows series for Kelly-Springfield tires, circa 1920. Daring use of white space gets the advertiser five times as much attention as he would achieve by filling the entire area with frantic, overcrowded, overanxious type talk. The caption antedated *The New Yorker* one-line cartoon caption practice by several years.

All that castle and all those windows and that tiny bit of utterly delightful conversation in the uppermost tower. Who could resist Carrier air conditioning after this? (AGENCY: *N. Y. Ayer & Son, Inc.*)

Lemon.

This Volkswagen missed the boat.

The chrome strip on the glove compartment is blemished and must be replaced. Chances are you wouldn't have noticed it; Inspector Kurt Kroner did.

There are 3,389 men at our Wolfsburg factory with only one job: to inspect Volkswagens at each stage of production. (3000 Volkswagens are produced daily; there are more inspectors than cars.)

Every shock absorber is tested (spot checking won't do), every windshield is scanned. VWs have been rejected for surface scratches barely visible to the eye.

Final inspection is really something! VW inspectors run each car off the line onto the Funktionsprüfstand (car test stand), tote up 189 check points, gun ahead to the automatic brake stand, and say "no" to one VW out of fifty.

This preoccupation with detail means the VW lasts longer and requires less maintenance, by and large, than other cars. (It also 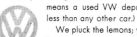 means a used VW depreciates less than any other car.)

We pluck the lemons; you get the plums.

William Bernbach, whose agency, Doyle Dane Bernbach Inc., produced this ad, says of it: "It was a ruthless VW inspector who considered this particular car a lemon because it had an almost invisible scratch somewhere on the door." Leading with the word "Lemon," the agency wrote this ad to prove once again that here indeed was an honest car. The Volkswagen series is perhaps the most outstanding "humorous" series in American advertising in current decades.

*PLUS TAX ©1959, BUXTON, INC. SPRINGFIELD, MASS.

Note the neatly shirred leather of this lady-like French Purse. It will expand like the proverbial squirrel's cheeks – to hold *all* your little niceties and necessities. Yet it never looks bulky. Choose red, light blue, black or antique white. $5.00*

An elegant place to store things:
Shirred French Purse by **LADY BUXTON**
best for your money

Another honey from Doyle Dane Bernbach is this Lady Buxton purse ad—pure joy in concept and execution. Imagine the difficulty of posing this photograph or the ingenuity of combining a couple of shots to achieve this joyous effect. (Mrs. Herold takes all the wind out of my sail by averring that the squirrel is stuffed.) —d.h.

LIBERAL TRADE-IN

bring in your wife
and just a few dollars
...we will give you a new woman

Ohrbach's

NEW YORK • NEWARK • LOS ANGELES

"A BUSINESS IN MILLIONS...
A PROFIT IN PENNIES"

Why cheat yourself of the
newest and best just because you
think you can't afford it? At Ohrbach's,
you don't have to pay high prices for beautiful
things. And there are tremendous assortments
to choose from — all new, all exciting. Bring us
the wife you have now and we will transform
her into a lovely new woman —
for just a few dollars. It will be
the easiest payment you ever made!

NEW YORK, 14th ST. FACING UNION SQUARE • IN NEWARK, MARKET & HALSEY STS.

Still another from the bell-ringing agency of Doyle
Dane Bernbach. William Bernbach says of this: "We
received many telegrams insisting that we live up to our
promise."

"So where's your bump of direction now?"

There always *is* a time when nothing but a Rand McNally Road Atlas will settle the family difference of opinion. And Dad has left it at home, depending on his bump of direction to keep him on the right road. Bumps, he can now tell you, are not dependable directors.

Experienced excursionists avoid such confusion by refusing to budge from home without a Rand McNally Road Atlas. They find it a dependable guide to the highways of the United States, southern Canada, and Mexico. It contains large two-color maps of each state, showing main roads and connecting highways. More than just a "book of maps," your Rand McNally Road Atlas includes descriptions of places of interest. Merely to read it starts a mental travelogue rolling.

And when it comes to actually setting out on a journey, you'll find the Automatic Route Finder will point an unwavering finger at the place you want to go. It will show the best and quickest routes between starting point and stopping point.

Priced at only $1.00, the new 1946 Rand McNally Road Atlas is available at most book, department, and stationery stores and at newsstands. Start planning your trip with a Rand McNally Road Atlas today.

RAND McNALLY & COMPANY
Established 1856

NEW YORK • CHICAGO • SAN FRANCISCO • WASHINGTON
Schoolbooks • School Maps • Children's Books • Road Maps
Travel Folders • Tickets • Coupon Books • Maps • Atlases
Globes • Bankers Monthly • Bankers Directory

Rand McNally could have used a realistic picture of their road atlas here, but how much more attention-getting and sales-making is this use of a familiar mapless family motoring situation. After reading this ad, no father will want to get himself into this "I told you so" predicament. (AGENCY: *Needham, Louis and Brorby, Inc.*)

You're never too old to travel

Some of the grandfather clocks we've moved were ancient. We handled them with respect—removed their pendulums, immobilized their works, protected them with thick quilted padding. And delivered them with their dignity intact. If this kind of extra care appeals to you, see the phone book for your Allied mover.

There's nothing we can imagine as difficult to pack and ship, and nothing as precious to preserve, as a grandfather clock. It's hard to conceive of a moving company with charm, but Allied Van Lines has achieved it here—humorously, sentimentally, and convincingly—in this comparatively small-space one-column ad. (AGENCY: *Young & Rubicam, Inc.*)

Casting around for good looks at low cost?

YOU CAN HAVE both good looks and low cost when you print on Management Bond. It's a low-priced watermarked sheet you can use with confidence.

Management Bond keeps jobs moving through the print shop. Its lint-free surface gives smooth feeding at high speeds, holds ink well—comes off the presses with clean crisp look. Take your choice of Management Bond in six colors and white and in standard weights and sizes.

And the uniform surface of Management Bond takes neat, readable typing —erases cleanly and easily.

Ask your printer to show you samples of Management Bond.

...specify MANAGEMENT BOND

MANAGEMENT BOND
A HAMMERMILL PRODUCT

On the Pacific Coast you can obtain **Management Bond** from the following Hammermill Agents:

Zellerbach Paper Company in San Francisco • Emeryville San Jose • Fresno • Los Angeles • San Diego • Sacramento Stockton • Portland • Eugene • Walla Walla • Seattle Spokane • Standard Paper Company in Tacoma.

Paper is hard to illustrate, especially when you're selling one kind of paper on another kind *of* paper! So Hammermill came to me, through B. B. D. & O. of Cleveland, to bring nonsense to bear, but relevantly, on the quality-plus-economy of Management Bond, in this ad used in several business publications.—*d.h.*

"A good cigar is as great a comfort to a man as a good cry is to a woman."
Lytton

CIGAR INSTITUTE OF AMERICA, INC.

This ad of the Cigar Institute of America is a masterpiece of simplicity and emotional appeal. The quote is captivating, and I don't quite know whether to cry, to kiss the girl's tear away, or to light a cigar. I guess I'll do all three. —*d.h.* (AGENCY: *David J. Mendelsohn Advertising Agency, Inc.*; PHOTOGRAPHER: *Robert Monroe*)

Is Tamiment the thinking man's St. Tropez?

All St. Tropez has is a smidgen of the Mediterranean. Tamiment has a whole lake of its own. And several Poconos of its own. And an 18-hole golf course of its own. And a theatre of its own. And two orchestras, and 18 tennis courts, and ballet, and bossa nova, and a big yellow moon. Tamiment (which sounds like a flavor) is a resort *with* a flavor. For a taste, call REctor 2-3050.

Tamiment
in the Poconos. Tamiment 5, Pennsylvania

All Sports Festival—June 7 thru 9
Competition's fierce, but the accent is on *fun.* Prizes for all participants—win, lose, or draw. P.S. Square dancing!

If Berman is the only Shelley you know, don't vacation at Tamiment.

At Tamiment-in-the-Poconos, Shelley is something you read while canoeing. Browning is delightful under Tamiment's sparkling sun. And we have 18 courts to play Tennyson. Tamiment (which sounds like a flavor) is a resort *with* a flavor. For a taste, call REctor 2-3050.

Tamiment
in the Poconos. Tamiment 5, Pennsylvania

Here's a resort I want to visit, just because its ads are smart, sassy, and sophisticated. The humor gives me the idea I won't be surrounded by stuffpots, and the typography sells class better than a full-page photo of the hotel in *The New Yorker.* These ads stand out like sunbeams in the murky mess of pages of resort advertising in New York newspapers. (AGENCY: *Redmond & Marcus*)

Do all wives go crazy when they get a BEAUTYREST ADJUSTABLE?

Not all of them, says Mr. Simmons. Just the smartest ones. Get a Beautyrest® Adjustable Bed and see. It's no time at all before a wife figures it out: Put your feet up where the head ought to be, and you've got a beauty treatment. Tired feet cool off. Puffy ankles resume their *wolf-whistle-ability*. Pale faces resume better-

than-makeup color. *The tricks these women know!* Occasionally, one *does* use Beautyrest Adjustable in orthodox fashion. Punch a button—up go knees. Or shoulders.

Or both. Eat breakfast in bed, watch TV, knit, read. Write nasty letters to Editors. Contoured or flat, you're *always* cradled on Beautyrest springs. Each spring lifts individu-

ally, so your back, et cetera, get *floating* support. No sags. No lumps. Oh, yes. Sometimes people who are ailing are advised to get an Adjustable Beautyrest, and from then on—*poof*. They're spoiled for life.

Beautyrest Adjustable Bed is a complete bed—including mattress and springs. Fits any standard bedstead or adjustable frame. Twin size, normal or extra-firm with dual motor, $379.50. Single motor, $279.50. Pneumatic, $189.50.

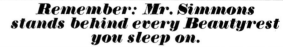

Remember: Mr. Simmons stands behind every Beautyrest you sleep on.

Simmons Beautyrest has succeeded in its advertising because it often has a sense of humor as well as a sense of beauty. Here's a high-priced mattress ($189.50 to $379.50), the Beautyrest Adjustable, which they sell with especially light-vein copy. (AGENCY: *Young & Rubicam, Inc.*)

by don herold

WIDTH of sleep
gives you DEPTH of sleep

If you don't collide with your partner during your night's sleep, you'll sleep more soundly.

Experts say the average sleeper turns over 25 times in his night's sleep. On an ordinary double mattress this means you may bump and perhaps waken yourself and bedmate 25 times.

It's depth of sleep that counts, not time. Seven hours on a Beautyrest King size (24 inches wider, 5 inches longer) or Queen size (6 inches wider, 5 inches longer) is worth 9 hours on a conventional mattress. (Half the usual double mattress is 27 inches—just the width of your baby crib.)

Bring your spine and your spouse in today and try one of the Beautyrest beauties for width and comfort (due to about 900 independent spring coils).

STORE NAME

In dealers' newspaper ads Simmons Beautyrest often goes to cartoons and text, because they know that cartoon ads come off the victor in the hurly-burly of mad, mad newspaper ad display in competition with supermarkets, second-hand car dealers, and department stores. (Incidentally, Tuesday is a good day for newspaper ads because the stores haven't started to go crazy for the weekend.)

Go-to-hell money:

In this enlightened year

of 1960

how about a word to

graduates they'll never hear

from the Commencement podium?

Not an inspirational word—

a bare-knuckle practical word.

In a few years, your wife

is going to say,

"It's 3 a.m., Harold, why

aren't you asleep?"

And you'll tell her how you're

stymied on your job and would

like to tell your boss to

go to hell.

She says, *"Why don't you?"*

And you list the reasons:

Rent;

Payments on the car;

Harold, Jr.;

Light, Gas, Insurance, etc.

So while the Grand March from

Aida is still ringing in your

ears, young man,

Decide to lay away some money

for the day you do tell your boss

...or the day he tells you!

This message is from

It took a sense of humor and some courage for *Newsweek* to address this shock message to college graduates and others on the subject of saving money. Not a word about *Newsweek*, but plenty of value to the magazine in this show of public service, good sense, and audacious informality.

Only type of executive chair we don't make

Model 6051 UA in
Flame Bedford Cord.

THAT'S BECAUSE WE SPECIALIZE IN BUSINESS FURNITURE. *The old-fashioned rocker has its merits, to be sure, but it's a back-breaker behind a desk. If you spend many long hours in an office, you'll enjoy the day-in, day-out comfort of Goodform executive chairs. There are many styles to choose from, all embodying the famous Goodform Principle of Adjustable Seating. For a free trial in your own office, call your nearby GF branch or dealer. Or write Dept. US-22 for chair literature. The General Fireproofing Company, Youngstown 1, Ohio.*

GF
BUSINESS FURNITURE

Cashing in humorously on the fame brought to rocking chairs by President Kennedy and his backache—an example of the punch to be gained by riding the news, or hooking up legitimately with something eminently in the public mind. Simplicity of layout, too, lends sock to this ad. What more can you ask of any ad than sock and rock? (AGENCY: *The Griswold-Eshleman Co.;* COPYWRITER: *E. M. Marker;* ART DIRECTOR: *Clayton Kenney*)

Land Sakes!
I do believe
I'll try one

—*they all keep saying*.. THEY'RE MILDER
—*and I hear them say*.. THEY TASTE BETTER

© 1935, LIGGETT & MYERS TOBACCO CO.

A sweet, human, humorous ad for Chesterfield, going back to
1935—years ahead of its time, blessed with simplicity, white space,
and irresistible human interest.

HOUSE AD

Our company is a lot like the house you see—roomy, very American, sort of funny looking from the outside—but comfortable and a good place to grow in. At least our present clients will tell you as much.

Even so, we admit it takes a heap o' ad-writin' to make a house a home, also a heap o' art directin', TV-producin', media-buyin', marketin', etc. But we do all those things, *and we try to do them all with a little extra guimpe.*

(The only thing that gives us trouble is the storm windows.)

LEO BURNETT COMPANY, INC., *Advertising*
CHICAGO • NEW YORK • HOLLYWOOD • TORONTO • MONTREAL

Advertising agencies tell me the hardest ads they have to write are their own house ads. (It's too much like a doctor doing his own appendectomy.) Only a few agencies have succeeded in getting anything but the most forbidding solemnity into their own ads. Leo Burnett Company, Inc., is one which has touched its own advertising with some merriment, and this house ad is one of many they've done for themselves in a happy vein.

Add a bowlful of people to the readers of your ad

Suppose you take a page in Life Magazine. Circulation, 7,000,000. Readership, 31,000,000 adults. An increase in the readers of your ad by one-fifth of 1% of that audience just about fills the Yale Bowl! A small increase in readership and persuasiveness may not look impressive on a sheet of statistics. But in flesh-and-blood people, it is. An outstanding agency doesn't settle even for a fine readership rating, but is always looking for more—a big percentage or even the little increase that still adds a bowlful of people. **Young & Rubicam, Advertising**

Young & Rubicam is another agency which has done its own house ads with warm humor and complete lack of customary heavy house ad pomposity. This particular ad happens to be dramatically graphic rather than entirely humorous. But come to think of it, it's really funny that nobody ever before used this way of showing the difference between the readership of a good ad in a good big magazine and that of just a mine-run ad in the same magazine.

GOLDILOCKS-UP-TO-DATE

(with a moral for medium-size advertisers)

First, Goldilocks tried the Papa Bear's bed. "Oh, my," she protested, "this bed is far too big."

You tend to get lost in a giant agency. Unless, of course, you happen to be a giant yourself.

Next, Goldilocks tried the Baby Bear's bed.

(A switch on the original, but we have a point to make.)

"Mercy," sighed Goldilocks, "this bed is just too tiny."

A small agency isn't the answer, either...not if you want everything from market research to P.R.

Finally, as you may have surmised, Goldilocks tried the Mama Bear's bed, "Crazy!" came her gleeful cry. "I mean this is cool!"

Do choose a place where you know you'll be comfortable.*

BUCHEN ADVERTISING, INC.

400 West Madison Street, Chicago
730 Fifth Avenue, New York
South Orange Federal Bldg., So. Orange, N. J.

*Of our forty accounts, the largest bills $1,500,000, the average is $300,000

This charming house ad by the Buchen Agency would get my business if my account were "medium-size."

as long as you're up get me a Grant's®

Please. It's the Scotch with the 8 on it. Under the Dufy. Why do they call it Grant's 8? That's the age. Most Scotch is only four years old, but it really takes 8 years to smooth out a Scotch. Water? A little. Thank you, darling.

The light and legendary 8-year-old blended Scotch Whisky. Eighty-six proof. Imported to the United States from Scotland by Austin, Nichols & Co., Inc., New York.   © 1962 Austin, Nichols & Co., Inc.

"As long as you're up" is a common phrase in most homes—and recognized and accepted happily as humorous if there is a sense of humor in the home. So it makes an instantly appealing headline for this Grant's Scotch ad. (AGENCY: *Hockaday Associates, Inc.*)

Tired of Playing Nursemaid
to a furnace ?

If you only realized the truth about a General Electric Oil Furnace — how wonderful it is, how easily installed, how much money it saves — you'd never put up with old-fashioned heat another day.

THERE'S never been anything like this G-E furnace. It's not just another oil burner— not an attachment you stick in an old furnace never intended for oil fuel,—but a complete coordinated unit—developed by G-E engineers after five years' work.

So good looking is this G-E Oil Furnace, so free from noise and dirt and smell that it converts your cellar into an extra room. And once it is in your home you can dismiss furnace tending problems entirely. As automatically as your lungs supply the right amount of oxygen to your blood stream, this furnace supplies the right amount of heat to your heating system.

The same is true of your hot water supply, for built in as a part of this furnace is a hot water heater that gives you a plentiful supply, winter or summer, most economically. In the summer only the water is heated.

You rarely go near this furnace, yet its "human brain"—the G-E Thermal Control—orders just the temperature you want—and gets it—day or night.

The efficiency of this furnace is so great, thanks to its unique design, that owners save 20% to 50% on what they

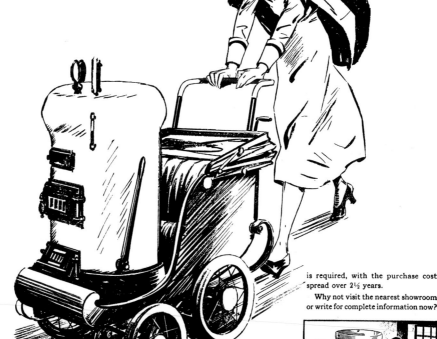

formerly spent for fuel every year.

Here are some of the unusual features that put the G-E Furnace in a class by itself: Flame burns downward instead of upward; all heat trapped; each drop of oil atomized by "impact expansion" into a hundred million particles—produces more heat from each drop and uses cheaper oil; boiler

made of heavy steel boiler plate, arc-welded, no joints to leak; all controls built in.

There is no need to wait to enjoy the comfort and economy of this great furnace. In one day, before your house cools off, you can have it installed—under the supervision of G-E trained engineers. Only a small down payment

is required, with the purchase cost spread over 2½ years.

Why not visit the nearest showroom or write for complete information now?

This furnace is a complete heating unit—burner, boiler, water heater and controls designed and made by G-E

GENERAL ⊕ ELECTRIC OIL FURNACE

Also on exhibition at the Architects Samples Corp., 101 Park Avenue, New York City

**SCHWERIN AIR
CONDITIONING CORP.**
570 Lexington Ave., N. Y. C.
2303 Grand Concourse, Bronx
138 E. Post Rd., White Plains
271 North Ave., New Rochelle

**AIR CONDITIONING
CORP.**
382 Central Ave., Newark, N. J.
217 Market St., Paterson, N. J.
47 Monmouth St., Red Bank, N. J.

ALFRED L. HART
82 Railroad Ave., Patchogue, L. I.
Showrooms at
11 E. Merrick Rd., Freeport
390 New York Ave., Huntington
209 W. Main St., Bayshore
67 Fulton St., W. Hempstead
381 Sunrise Highway, Lynbrook
51 Hill St., Southampton

**AUTOMATIC
APPLIANCE CORP.**
51 River Street, Stamford, Conn.

GENE MEENAN, INC.
Flatbush Ave. Extension, Corner Willoughby
St., Brooklyn
80 Bay St., St. George, Staten Island
164-07 Hillside Ave., Jamaica, L. I.
59-08 Woodside Ave., Woodside, L. I.

PHILLIPS & IBSEN, INC.
69 South Broadway, Nyack, N. Y.

**L. C. KELLEY
SALES CO.**
183 Fairfield Ave., Bridgeport, Conn.

GENERAL ELECTRIC AIR CONDITIONING FOR WINTER, SUMMER AND YEAR ROUND

CLIP AND MAIL COUPON TODAY

GENERAL ELECTRIC CO.,
Air Conditioning Dept., Div. H. T. 3-25
570 Lexington Avenue, New York City

Please send me further information about the General Electric Oil Furnace, without obligation on my part.

Name . . . .

Residence . . . .

City . . . . *State* . . . .

Gentle spoofing condemnation of old-fashioned furnaces (woman killers) in favor of General Electric electric heating units.

KELLOGG'S INVITES THE KIDS TO MAKE THE ADS

Reva Rice, Newcombe, Kentucky, drew a comparison for her ad.

How would you like to do what 9-year-old Reva did—make a Kellogg's Corn Flakes ad for a magazine and win a $100 U. S. Savings Bond, too!

Well, if you're 14 years or less, you can try for this big thrill. All you do is make an ad showing what you like best about Kellogg's Corn Flakes.

Maybe you want to show their freshness. Or crispness. Perhaps you think they're a world favorite because their flavor has never been duplicated. Or

you may have some altogether new and different idea.

Read the rules on a Kellogg's Corn Flakes package and get started with your crayons or paints today. Remember, if your ad is used over the air or in a magazine, you'll get a $100 U. S. Savings Bond . . . plus a $500 Bond if it's judged one of the year's top six!

Every entrant gets this pin.

FRESH FROM KELLOGG'S OF BATTLE CREEK
the CRISP, CRISP flakes with the DEEP, DEEP flavor!

Says James D. Woolf in *Advertising Age:* "Corn flakes are pretty much a staple product, too, but this hurdle did not stop the Leo Burnett agency from coming up with a new and different expression, completely cliché-free, of the theme that Kellogg's Corn Flakes are delicious and healthful. I refer to the advertisements written by kids and illustrated with their childish but delightful drawings."

Is it possible? Panties more comfortable than wearing nothing!

This may come as a shock, but—Eiderlon panties actually <u>are</u> more comfortable than wearing nothing. Even <u>more</u> comfortable than wearing most anything else. How is it possible? Eiderlon, the wonderblend knit fabric of finest combed cotton and rayon, is incredibly soft, incredibly absorbent. Result? You never feel sticky, clammy or uncomfortable...whatever the weather Eiderlon "vibrancy" makes whites whiter...colors and prints bloom. Machine-washable and dryable. Look for Eiderlon panties and sleepwear at fine stores.

eiderlon®

Spun-lo Eiderlon, Inc., 500 Fifth Avenue, New York 36, N.Y.

This ad has everything—a pretty young mother wearing nothing from her panties up (that may be sex), a nude baby (which isn't sex), and incomparably good humor in the headline.

"Advertising never sold me anything!"

We've all heard that one before. Often.

But it's not true.

Fact is, whether we know it or not—or admit it or not—advertising has sold something to every one of us.

And that's all to the good.

In the first place, a basic function of advertising is to *inform*. To convey news. News about products. What they are. Where to get them. How much they cost. Through this function alone, advertising sells great quantities of goods.

Secondly—even people like the little lady above, who make a conscious effort to reject advertising, are made to *want* the things advertised. Sooner or later, that leads to a sale.

Finally, there is a third and much broader way in which advertising sells us things. It creates so much

demand that mass production is possible; hence, more goods are sold to more people for less money.

Yes, it's all to the good, because it makes the wheels go 'round. Advertising makes possible the high-speed distribution that is the key to our

---

ADVERTISING AS A SOCIAL FORCE

"Advertising nourishes the consuming power of men. It creates wants for a better standard of living. It sets up before a man the goal of a better home, better clothing, better food for himself and his family. It spurs individual exertion and greater production. . . . The business of advertising has a big part to play in the future of the world."

– from a speech by Sir Winston Churchill, delivered before the Advertising Club of London, 1924

---

economic system. Without it, capitalism as we know it would be impossible.

So, Madam, think what you will. Meanwhile, you can keep enjoying the things made available because of advertising's vast contribution to our economic and social system.

And *say* what you will, Madam. It's a free country! And that freedom, too, is part of the great tradition of which advertising is a very real part.

☆　　☆　　☆

Advertising is our business, and we take pride in it. As one of America's ten largest agencies, we are grateful to play a part, along with our clients, in the dynamic growth of the world's economy.

BENTON & BOWLES, INC.
666 Fifth Avenue, New York
Advertising and Marketing counsel to leaders in American business

Benton & Bowles' answer to this sassy little old spinster is, "The heck it hasn't!" and they adequately squash her in the above copy. A good agency house ad, incidentally, because in it Benton & Bowles are content to lay claim to being one of the ten largest companies helping the American economy by producing advertising that produces mass production.

Why doesn't the Sow's Ear Silk Purse Co. advertise, Andy?

They know sows' ears won't stand spotlight

don herold

ADVERTISERS CAN'T ADVERTISE AND HIDE, TOO

ADVERTISERS can't advertise and then beat it. They have to hang around a while to cash in.

Peanut carts don't advertise. Gold brick foundries don't advertise. (Policemen can read, can't they?)

If an advertiser spends a small fortune to tell the world where he is, it's only common sense for him to *be there*. And be there with the goods.

A little quiet dishonesty might pay a business, but you can't tell lies on a big scale. Somebody in the audience is going to squeak.

The mere magnitude and sheer cost of a big national advertising campaign purifies the product advertised and fumigates the organization behind it. Big scale advertisers cannot afford big scale comebacks. They know if they start out to *tell the world* they had better tell the world *straight*.

Advertising costs so much these days that there's hardly any advertising now to make single sales. It pays only when it starts an avalanche of satisfaction. If you see somebody advertising right along, you know the goods are delivering the goods.

Andy Consumer

THE NATIONAL ADVERTISER BETS HIS ADVERTISING MONEY THAT HIS PRODUCT IS RIGHT

For several years I took great pleasure in trying to help explain advertising's economic functions to consumers in a monthly series signed by one of them "Andy Consumer" in the early *Life* magazine—another way of saying the same thing expressed on the preceding page in the good ad by Benton & Bowles. —*d.h.*

A Hog Can Cross America Without Changing Trains—But YOU Can't!

The Chesapeake & Ohio and the Nickel Plate Road again propose to give humans a break!

It's hard to believe, but it's true.

If you want to ship a hog from coast to coast, he can make the entire trip without changing cars. You can't. It is impossible for you to pass through Chicago, St. Louis, or New Orleans without breaking your trip!

There is an invisible barrier down the middle of the United States which you cannot cross without inconvenience, lost time, and trouble.

560,000 Victims in 1945!

If you want to board a sleeper on one coast and ride through to the other, you must make double Pullman reservations, pack and transfer your baggage, often change stations, and wait around for connections.

It's the same sad story if you make a relatively short trip. You can't cross that mysterious line! To go from Fort Wayne to Milwaukee or from Cleveland to Des Moines, you must also stop and change trains.

Last year alone, more than 560,000 people were forced to make annoying, time-wasting stopovers at the phantom Chinese wall which splits America in half!

End the Secrecy!

Why should travel be less convenient for people than it is for pigs? Why should Americans be denied the benefits of through train service? No one has yet been able to explain it.

Canada has this service . . . with a choice of two routes. Canada isn't split down the middle. Why should we be? No reasonable answer has yet been given. Passengers still have to stop off at Chicago, St. Louis, and New Orleans—although they can ride right through other important rail centers.

It's time to pry the lid off this mystery. It's time for action to end this inconvenience to the public . . . NOW!

Many railroads could cooperate to provide this needed through service. To date, the Chesapeake & Ohio and the Nickel Plate ALONE have made a public offer to do so.

How about it!

Once more we would like to go on record with this specific proposal:

The Chesapeake & Ohio, whose western passenger terminus is Cincinnati, stands ready now to join with any combination of other railroads to set up connecting transcontinental and intermediate service through Chicago and St. Louis, on practical schedules and routes.

The Nickel Plate Road, which runs to Chicago and St. Louis, also stands ready now to join with any combination of roads to set up the same kind of connecting service through these two cities.

Through railroad service can't be blocked forever. The public wants it. It's bound to come. Again, we invite the support of the public, of railroad people and railroad investors—for this vitally needed improvement in rail transportation!

Chesapeake & Ohio Railway • Nickel Plate Road

Terminal Tower, Cleveland 1, Ohio

One of the most famous humorous ads ever printed. The late Robert Young made the Chicago wall (for passenger trains) as infamous as the Berlin wall has become (for people). The situation still exists, and it is still almost too serious to be humorous.

Frank Case was not only an artist at running a hotel in New York, but he could write well enough to put its personality into several books and into his advertising copy. In this ad he recognizes the universal human liking for being known by name. The touch of Frank Case made the Algonquin Hotel *the* favorite of writers, artists, actors, and celebrities in all fields for many decades.

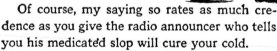
Billy Rose, millionaire, showman, theatre owner and, I believe, the largest single owner of A.T.&T. stock, was one of the best advertising copywriters in America in his series for his erstwhile Diamond Horseshoe. Imagine a night club owner saying, "I don't know why anyone should want to go to a night club, but . . ."

IF YOU MUST GO NORTH
...FLY UNITED!

Most jets to Pittsburgh and Cleveland

You can take a swift United 720 Jet Mainliner® nonstop to Pittsburgh at 12:30 p.m. or to Cleveland at 2:45 p.m. Our 2:00 p.m. jet goes 1-stop to Pittsburgh, then on to Cleveland. And United offers Caravelle jet service to both cities daily.

Nonstop SKY-BUS to Pittsburgh, onestop to Cleveland

Only United offers "bus" service nonstop to Pittsburgh and one-stop to Cleveland. Two departures daily, 8:55 a.m. & 11:20 p.m.

Only service to Buffalo and Rochester

Thrifty coach flights to Buffalo daily — no-change-of-plane service to Rochester.

Ask about our new 15% saving on round-trips. See your Travel Agent or call United at FR 7-3461 — at your service, 7 days a week, 24 hours a day.

UNITED

THE EXTRA CARE AIRLINE

A winning ad appearing in a January issue of the *Miami Herald*. Appealing because it hits home with anybody contemplating the unpleasant prospect of going north from Florida into freezing weather, and even, in many cases, the problem of borrowing a warm overcoat (and mittens) for the trip. (AGENCY: *N. W. Ayer & Son, Inc., Chicago;* ARTIST: *Ted Carr;* COPYWRITER: *Charles P. Bolmar*)

BOWLER BY JAMES LOCK & COMPANY, LTD., LONDON, ENGLAND—CREATORS OF THE FIRST BOWLER HAT.

Two historic inventions that Englishmen still hold dear

Above, left, an Englishman's favourite headgear—the bowler. Above, right, an Englishman's favourite gin—Gordon's. The bowler made its first appearance in 1855, a full 86 years *after* Alexander Gordon had introduced his remarkable gin. The Gordon's Gin you drink today still harks back to the original 1769 English formula. Why tamper with such dryness and flavour? They have made Gordon's the biggest-selling gin in all of England, America, the world.

PRODUCT OF U.S.A. DISTILLED LONDON DRY GIN, 100% NEUTRAL SPIRITS DISTILLED FROM GRAIN. 90 PROOF. GORDON'S DRY GIN CO. LTD., LINDEN, NEW JERSEY

Pleasant humor in mock dignity, imparting grandiose historical significance to two English institutions, the bowler and Gordon's Gin. Captivating in its simplicity. (AGENCY: *Grey Advertising Agency, Inc.;* PHOTOGRAPHER: *O. Paccione*)

A SQUEAKY GRAIN WAGON bringing a neighbor's grain to Jack Daniel's Hollow is about the only thing that ever stirs up our ducks.

What attracts ducks to the Hollow is our spillings of fine grains and cool, iron-free water. But what keeps them here is our quiet, unhurried way of life. You see, we still make old-fashioned Tennessee whiskey just the way Jack Daniel always did. That calls for slowly Charcoal Mellowing it to a *sippin'* smoothness. And that "extra blessing" takes too much care and patience for much bustling around.

CHARCOAL
MELLOWED

DROP

BY DROP

© 1961, Jack Daniel Distillery, Lem Motlow, Prop., Inc.

TENNESSEE WHISKEY · 90 PROOF BY CHOICE · DISTILLED AND BOTTLED BY JACK DANIEL DISTILLERY · LYNCHBURG (POP. 384), TENN.

If you have supreme quality in your merchandise, you need have no fear of using humor in your advertising, as testified in this veritable masterpiece of photography and copywriting for Jack Daniels whiskey. I'd have been as proud of writing this copy as I would have been of doing one of Shakespeare's sonnets. —*d.h.* (AGENCY: *Gardner Advertising Company, St. Louis;* COPYWRITER: *Bill Weston;* PHOTOGRAPHER: *Joe Clark*)

Who ate my Post Toasties?

Practically <u>nothing</u> is worse than finding the Post Toasties box empty, and having a back turned on your problem. Especially since Post Toasties are the <u>only</u> corn flakes with that rustly-rich, super-tasting flavor. So hurry to the store, Mom, and tell the man you want some more. For goodness sake — get **Post Toasties!**

A Product of General Foods

Family tragedy—Post Toasties all gone—dramatically but happily drawn by always-sophisticated cartoonist Whitney Darrow, Jr. Much better than the usual "Yum! Yum!" situation. (AGENCY: *Benton & Bowles, Inc.*)

Suddenly it's not quite spring

Hark, hark, the lark, and all those nice things. The birds are on the wing. And we thought you ought to know that the Green Giant has taken off his galoshes and come down with a fine case of pre-spring fever.

He gets positively giddy every year this time. Wants to fly South to meet the robins halfway, and things like that. The reason he has spring fever right now instead of later, as most sensible people have, is because he's so busy next month he just can't work it in.

You see, comes April, comes pea-planting time. When the frost is out of the ground and warm, little breezes start flitting about, that's when the Green Giant swings into action.

That special pedigreed seed has to be planted on just the right day. Then, as soon as the pea plants poke their heads above ground, he starts fussing like a brand-new father. He checks the soil, the temperature, the rainfall, and heaven knows what. You'd think he was growing emeralds.

When Green Giant Brand peas are out of the fields and into the cans we're more worn out than he is. Mind you, he's not an easy giant to live with all through this. But everyone tiptoes around and is very patient with him. After all, we're glad he takes his work seriously. And so are lots of other people. Why don't you eat some of his nice vegetables?

For many years, Leo Burnett has been selling Green Giant peas with fun. Peas are not very photogenic, either in the pod, in a can or in a saucer, and you can't rhapsodize too wildly about them. So the Burnett agency really found a swell way out when they invented and personalized the Green Giant.

Ingratiating deviation of the ads for Green Giant corn. Too long to be read by everybody, but thoroughly charming in its kidding of McGuffy moralizing and its ridiculing of conventional advertising of the oversentimental school. It's therefore utterly effective with those who have a few moments to read. It could have been done differently, more conventionally and less effectively with a stickily sentimental picture of a consumer eating Niblets, with a dream insert of his dear old mother serving corn on the cob, with perhaps a "Yum! Yum" or two thrown in to insure nausea. (AGENCY: *Leo Burnett Company, Inc.*)

Judge isn't mad about anything!

Of course, there *are* a lot of things that get on Judge's nerves.

For instance, there is the hard life that circus zebras are made to live. A lady once called our attention to it. They have to get up early in the morning, march in the parade, stand up and emphasize their stripes at two performances daily, travel all night on a train without any sleep —and do the same thing all over again the next day. That makes Judge's blood boil.

And jimpson weeds! Oh, how Judge hates jimpson weeds — secretly

One time Judge made a list of the provoking things in the world, and there were 25,670,424,-231 of them. Then Judge studied all the available statistics on the possible production of white paper, and thought, "What's the use to try to reform the world with so little white paper at hand?"

Judge decided it would be much rarer just to try to be as pleasant as possible. Though that is a high mark to set. There are so few things left to be intelligently pleasant about.

Send a dollar for 13 trial weeks of Judge, and Judge will make only one condition. It has just got to make adverse mention now and then of—well, you know.

the nation's perpetual
smileage book

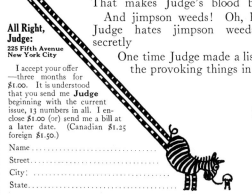

All Right, Judge:
225 Fifth Avenue
New York City

I accept your offer —three months for $1.00. It is understood that you send me **Judge** beginning with the current issue, 13 numbers in all. I enclose $1.00 (or) send me a bill at a later date. (Canadian $1.25 foreign $1.50.)

Name...........................
Street..........................
City:..........................
State..........................

It was fun to create irresponsible subscription ads for both old *Judge* and *Life* magazines, when America was young and foolish enough to support several humorous magazines. —d.h.

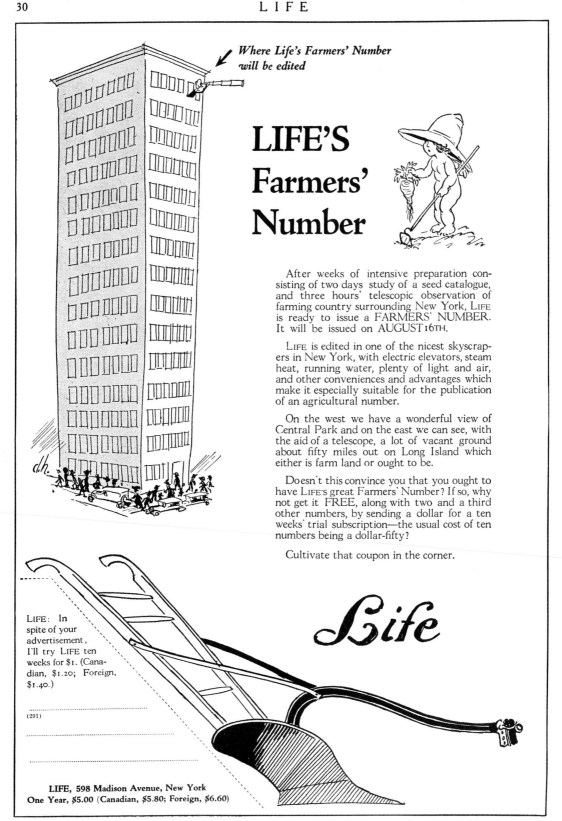

Where Life's Farmers' Number will be edited

LIFE'S Farmers' Number

After weeks of intensive preparation consisting of two days study of a seed catalogue, and three hours' telescopic observation of farming country surrounding New York, LIFE is ready to issue a FARMERS' NUMBER. It will be issued on AUGUST 16TH.

LIFE is edited in one of the nicest skyscrapers in New York, with electric elevators, steam heat, running water, plenty of light and air, and other conveniences and advantages which make it especially suitable for the publication of an agricultural number.

On the west we have a wonderful view of Central Park and on the east we can see, with the aid of a telescope, a lot of vacant ground about fifty miles out on Long Island which either is farm land or ought to be.

Doesn't this convince you that you ought to have LIFE'S great Farmers' Number? If so, why not get it FREE, along with two and a third other numbers, by sending a dollar for a ten weeks' trial subscription—the usual cost of ten numbers being a dollar-fifty?

Cultivate that coupon in the corner.

Life

LIFE: In spite of your advertisement, I'll try LIFE ten weeks for $1. (Canadian, $1.20; Foreign, $1.40.)

(291)

LIFE, 598 Madison Avenue, New York
One Year, $5.00 (Canadian, $5.80; Foreign, $6.60)

It's awful hard to pull a button off a Van Heusen shirt

Van Heusen really got its teeth into this problem, and put its laboratory experts to work. They tested buttons, tested threads, tested stitching, and finally found a way to make these fine pearl buttons really tug-proof. Nothing less would be good enough to match Van Heusen's quality sewmanship: smart new "comfort contour" collar styling; action-tailored shoulders, armholes, elbows; figure-tapered lines; fine, laboratory-tested, Sanforized fabrics in whites and exclusive patterns. A new shirt free if your Van Heusen shrinks out of size! If you want lots of gals hanging around, swing into a Van Heusen shirt. $3.50, $3.95, $4.95.

Phillips-Jones Corp., New York 1, N. Y. • Makers of Van Heusen Shirts • Ties • Pajamas • Collars • Sport Shirts

Almost too outlandish to be accepted, but where only a shirt button is involved, why demand too much logic? The line, "If you want lots of gals hanging around" kids the overuse of sex appeal in too many ads.

Inspiration vs. IBMism

For the first time we have an auditing approach to advertising. —ROSSER REEVES in *Reality in Advertising.*

Research has grown too big for its breeches. It will never, in the world of marketing, take the place of disciplined intuition. —E. B. WEISS

Carefulness is the laziest form of art.

I've known a number of artists who couldn't do anything very well, but who have tried to make up for it by doing it terrifically hard.

They meticulously draw every wrinkle in a coat sleeve, and they draw every blade of grass.

Lacking inspiration, they offer gallons of perspiration.

In advertising, I've noticed that many men without creative spark will throw up a smoke screen of surveys, research, statistics, and mathematics.

Rosser Reeves, in his book, *Reality in Advertising,* indicates that good advertising can be produced by IBM machines and copywriting robots—all easy to buy, rent, or hire.

But I believe that if you rule instinct and inspiration and art out of advertising creation, you rule out the very factors that make some campaigns ten times as effective as others.

In one of their house ads, Young & Rubicam, Inc., wrote: "The best advertisement in a magazine is something like five times as effective as the average advertisement and fourteen times as effective as the poorest."

I have often noticed that . . . well, let's take athletes. Ten guys on a football team may all be pretty good, but there is often one player who seems to stand out as being five times as spectacular as the others. It is not scientific coaching, or textbook study, or diagrams on a blackboard that make this fellow loom up super; it is a God-given instinctive talent for running faster, dodging more adroitly, performing more beautifully in every way. Tom Shevlin, famous football coach, has said:

It takes a certain amount of mania to accomplish anything beyond the ordinary routine. In playing football, the main thing is to go crazy. Two good men can handle any sane man, but it takes five to handle a crazy one. There are moments in every game, when, to win, you've got to be better than you know how to be, and you can't reach this point over any sane trail.

There's a certain amount of craziness in all good humorous advertising.

Some of the best research that a copywriter can do is within his own soul. Says Gerald Stanley Lee:

My own belief is that the man who succeeds best in tapping the subconscious in other people is the man who has the habit and the daily gift of surprising himself first—who knows how to escape from the almost universal disease in writing copy, of *calculate-itis*, who forgets about impressing other people, the man who has a perfectly splendid time with something in being impressed himself.

I believe the best advertising is not created by chained slaves in a copywriters' galley, but by folks who are having a circus at their jobs.

Leo Burnett, one of today's very best, and head of an agency so large and so good it must surprise him every morning, writes:

The biggest problem of all for an agency as large as ours, as I see it, is a human one—how to keep from *acting* big.

It is true that we must have more definite assignments of responsibility, more definite procedures, fixed policies and a generally tighter operation.

At the same time, however, if creative ideas are to flourish, I believe we must also preserve what I call a "spirit of fun." Nobody is in business for fun, but that does not mean there cannot be fun in business.

By fun, of course, I mean a friendly kind of humanness—a minimum of starchy shirts, protocol and formalized procedures.

When, God forbid, we become a "slick" advertising agency we won't be the same company any more, and I, for one, won't want to work here any more."

"The essence of advertising is to persuade and move people," says William Bernbach, president of Doyle Dane Bernbach Inc., most of whose campaigns have a delightful touch of humor (in the sense in which *I* mean humor). "Research is not going to do that for you. Marketing is not going to do that for you." He goes on to explain:

What is the use of saying all the right things in the world if nobody is going to read them? And, believe me, nobody is going to read them if they are not said with freshness, originality and imagination.

I plead for as much effort and thought and energy in the development of the art of saying things with the greatest effectiveness as you have put into the so-called practical aspects of your organization.

It is our belief that every other activity in our business is a prelude, however important, but just a prelude, to the final performance which is the ad; that the measure of that performance is its persuasion; and that persuasion is not a science easily learned like an equation, but an art that can reach inspired heights only by a deeply personal intuition.

Mark Twain once wrote that the difference between the right word and the almost right word is the difference between lightning and the lightning bug.

William Bernbach points out that the mere shooting of coins against walls of public indifference may eventually penetrate, but that this long and costly attack was a luxury which his agency and his clients at the beginning could not afford. "We had to make one ad do the work of ten."

So, did they yell and scream and hammer? No, their earlier work was marked by humor and quiet sell and freshness, and their present work still is.

Mr. Bernbach quotes Albert Einstein as follows: "The supreme task of the physicist is to arrive at those universal elementary laws from which the cosmos can be built up by pure deduction. There is no logical path to these laws; only intuition, resting on sympathetic understanding of experience, can reach them."

(Einstein, by the way, was a man with a great sense of humor. He was explaining his fondness for the little girl next door: "I help her with her arithmetic homework and she gives me some of her jelly beans.")

One of the best arguments I've ever read against grim determination in the creation of advertising concepts is this quotation from Robert R. Updegraff, author of the famous *Obvious Adams:*

Fehr, the French scientist, who made a study of the working habits of his contemporaries, says that 75 percent of the scientists stated that their important discoveries came to them when they were not actively engaged in research.

Most of us use our conscious minds entirely too hard, and as a result our thinking and our decisions are not as good as they should be. The trouble is, we are working with only half our minds, and with less than half of our accumulated experience and judgment. And as a consequence, we cheat ourselves of many hours of recreation which in themselves, add to the effectiveness of our thinking. *For relaxation is the key to the door of the subconscious mind.* The subconscious mind works best when we are doing what we like best to do. A happy mind is a healthy mind, and it puts drive back of a man's activities. As Henry David Thoreau put it, "A really efficient laborer will be found not to crowd his day with work."

Wernher von Braun said: "Research is what I do when I don't know what I'm doing."

British sailor before Vitamin C

On other pages I've reproduced some of Doyle Dane Bernbach's ads—among them one for Volkswagen and one for Ohrbach's. Here are Mr. Bernbach's comments in *Advertising Age* on these two ads:

You may remember a VW ad that simply showed a car with the headline, LEMON. You know that this is the classic description for disappointment in a car. Yet here it was used to prove memorably once again that here indeed was an honest car. For it was the ruthless VW inspector who considered this particular car a lemon because it had an almost invisible scratch somewhere on the door. Suppose we had merely said, "Every VW must pass rigid inspection." How many ads and how much money do you think it would have taken to make the same point that was made in one creative stroke with the one word headline, LEMON?

(The same light touch is carried through in radio commercials for Volkswagen. Example: "My daddy just bought a awful looking car called a Volkswagen. It's real little and has funny round fenders that don't stick out in back or anything.

There's just a hole where the motor ought to be, and the motor's where the trunk was. It's all just one color and there isn't any shiny grille in front at all. I guess daddy doesn't care what people think of us.

Of one of his agency's Ohrbach ads, Mr. Bernbach writes:

I remember one of the Ohrbach campaigns in which we were satirizing some popular advertising techniques. We had a man carrying a woman off the page under his arm. The headline shouted: "LIBERAL Trade-in, bring us your wife and just a few dollars and we will give you a new woman." We received many telegrams insisting that we live up to our promise.

If there ever was a classic example of the economy of creativity in advertising, this is it. Ohrbach's spends about one-thirtieth the amount spent by the biggest department store in New York.

I believe, of course, in using all scientific methods possible to determine in advance, or in trial runs, or afterwards, how effective campaign approaches are, but I've seen surveys come some terrible croppers in my time. Ford, for example, when gestating the Edsel, spent $250 million to learn exactly the kind of car the public wanted and to get ready to make it, and look what happened to Edsel! The right guy with a half hour's

British "Limey" after Vitamin C

study, could have told Ford to build a Rambler, or some form of low-priced compact, easy on gas and tires. Just a little bit of horse sense can frequently beat the pants off of hundreds of thousands of dollars' worth of MIT and IBM efforts to measure human expectations or reactions.

At the end of a recent calendar year it was easy to learn that Pall Malls sold "so many" billion and led the industry.

But even those figures do not tell you that Pall Mall might have sold 10 billion more if it had had commercials less silly than: "Pall Mall's famous length travels and gentles the smoke naturally—over, under, around and through Pall Mall's fine, mellow tobaccos."

No copywriter worth his salt writes without serious preliminary study of his products and their merchandising problems.

In one chapter of his book, Mr. Reeves says that the methods of *his* agency produce results for its customers 15.4 per cent better than the average of competing brands, and a usage pull 16.2 per cent higher.

This statement is so exact as to make me wonder. We often see exactitude made foolish in advertising with such statements as "Wonder Bread helps build strong bodies 12 ways!" The most classic of all exact statements in advertising was intentionally so precise that it revealed a redeeming touch of humor, that of Ivory Soap's "99-44/100% pure."

Nobody believed this, and nobody believed that Procter & Gamble believed it, but it was so humorously exact that it won billions of friends for Ivory Soap. Besides, Ivory Soap floated.

Norman B. Norman, president of Norman, Craig & Kummel Inc., insists that "the business of advertising is solely to move goods. You bastardize it if you try to make it an art form."

I insist that it is also the business of advertising to make friends for advertising and to drive nobody shrieking in retreat from it, even if they stop at the store and buy a package of your product on their way.

Two sagely skeptical evaluations of the worth of IBMism are: Henry Clay's "Statistics are no substitute for judgment" and Mark Twain's "Get your facts first, and then you can distort them as much as you please."

Perhaps Lin Yutang may be given the final word on this subject: "After all, only he who handles his ideas lightly is master of his ideas—and only he who is master of his ideas is not enslaved by them. Seriousness, after all, is only a sign of effort, and effort is a sign of imperfect mastery."

Somewhere from these men of wisdom I think we'll get our guidance for the attainment of long-range effectiveness in advertising, rather than from anybody's philosophy that we can succeed in commanding attention and making sales only by mastering mathematics and then committing public nuisance with them on a gigantic scale.

the nicest things happen
to people who carry....

Baddie

One mistake made by many advertisers attempting to use humor in advertising is that of getting completely outlandish. I think this series on First National City Bank traveler's checks does little to sell the sense or many conveniences of carrying National City traveler's checks. Who wants his baggage carried by a kangaroo? —*d.h.*

Sudan Batiste-on-the-Rocks by *Jayson*

Woven from PIMA long-staple cotton

It's the *ingredients* that count for smartness...coolness...good taste. JAYSON Sudan Batiste is as cool and lightweight as a fabric can be. PIMA long staple cotton gives JAYSON Sudan Batiste a natural, deep-seated lustre that actually improves with laundering. And, with JAYSON's "fit to perfection" tailoring, you'll always be neat and fresh though the days be hot or humid. This summer, enjoy batiste at its best...JAYSON Sudan Batiste. See it at your favorite store.

SPORT SHIRT...convertible collar. White, blue, maize, tan, green, grey. Short sleeves $3.95; long sleeves $4.95.

DRESS SHIRT...Jay-Mil collar illustrated. Also available in Carefree collar, short sleeves, or Button-down collar, long sleeves, $3.95. White, blue, tan, grey, green.

PAJAMA...illustrated, V-neck, short sleeves, knee length, $4.95. Not illustrated—convertible collar, long sleeves, long trousers, $5.95. White, blue, grey, green, maize, tan.

JAYSON, 1115 Broadway, New York 10, New York *Also makers of* Excello *Shirts and* Sport Shirts

Baddie

"Eye-patch" advertising carried to extremes. What appeal can there possibly be in the suggestion of sitting on an iceberg, or of even associating with one in short shirt sleeves? Just a nervous attempt to attract attention with a crazy illustration. Whimsy mechanically conceived, not born simply of the product. —*d.h.*

Baddie

Two lamentable trends in humorous advertising: (1) the use, in a strained effort to be modern, of monster-type characters (often with noses coming off the top of the heads, leaving no room for brains); (2) the use of obvious child-idiot types to express endorsement of the product. Here, in addition to the latter, the copy is affected to the point of being almost incomprehensible. —*d.h.*

*Du Pont trademark

A MAN
YOU CAN
LEAN ON
THAT'S
KLOPMAN

Because nobody makes better fabric than Klopman — and GLENEAGLES™ knows it. For this fully lined Bal Raglan style raincoat, Gleneagles chooses 80% "DACRON"* POLYESTER and 20% COTTON POPLIN. Tan olive, charcoal, black, brown or blue olive. Regulars, shorts, longs, extra longs. About $37.50. Weber & Heilbroner, New York; Muse's, Atlanta; Kennedy's, Boston & New England; Burkhardt's, Cincinnati; Wm. H. Block Co., Indianapolis; Magee's, Lincoln. KLOPMAN MILLS, INC., 450 Seventh Avenue, New York 1, N.Y.

Baddie

This gentleman has nothing to lean on, let alone strength or support or balance to allow somebody to lean *on him*. The unreasonableness of the suggestion diverts attention from any possible merits of Westchester Gleneagles raincoats of Klopman fabric. —*d.h.*

OIL'S WELL

that ends up in an Avis car. An Avis man fills up the tank, too -- all FREE from Avis for miles of non-stop driving. Next time you ponder the many ramifications of automotive engineering, think of free gas and oil...think Avis.

Baddie

Another use of the monster type of cartoon, and helped none by copy too obtuse to be comprehended by even the most intellectual motorist.

*"American Airlines, Inc. carries more passengers
than any other airline in the world."*

Baddie

A funny cartoon, but totally irrelevant to American Airlines, Inc. I would like the cartoon or the line of advertising copy, but feel that, together, they merely detract from each other. —*d.h.*

"Mrs. Gillberry was rather intent on a Hoover."

This is an advertisement (what else?)

Baddie

A situation so gruesome, that I can't possibly imagine it creating any kindly feeling for Hoover vacuum cleaners. —d.h.

The Covered Bridge at Cornwall, Connecticut

For a better way to take care of your nest egg talk to the people at Chase Manhattan

There's just no respite from financial ponderings for those who insist upon struggling with their own investments.

But it needn't happen to you.

Commission Chase Manhattan's Personal Trust Division to watch over your nest egg right away. Without fuss or feathers, sympathetic Chasemen will see to it that you're quit of such repetitive details as call dates, coupons and record keeping.

And at a word from you the Personal Trust Division will act as your Executor and Trustee, serve as Custodian of your securities, advise you on your investments and plan your estate with you and your lawyer.

Simply ring up the Personal Trust Division at LL 2-2222 or write 1 Chase Manhattan Plaza, New York 15, for an appointment.

THE CHASE MANHATTAN BANK

Baddie

Another overstrained effort to get attention, which in no way suggests any of the many fine advantages of establishing a relationship with The Chase Manhattan Bank Trust Division. —*d.h.*

Cartoons in Advertising

Cartoons sell goods for the same reasons that they win political campaigns, upset corrupt political rings and otherwise get results in public life.—D.H.

Cartoons are a medium for which there is universal friendship, and, in any advertising effort, it helps to start off among friends.

America is a land of balloon readers.

Since 1932, surveys of reading habits by Dr. George Gallup and others have established the fact that "next to one or more news stories and to full-page photo pages, more readers go for the cartoons than for anything else in the papers. This is as true of women readers as of men readers."

A cartoon is the antithesis of a blueprint. It suggests fun. It says (sometimes untruthfully): "Here at last is an advertiser who isn't going to be pompous."

It establishes an atmosphere of acceptance. (I've already defined humor as something that nature provides to enable us to stand the unbearable.) It opens our pores and opens our minds, and we loosen our clamps.

But I do not believe in the "funny sell."

A cartoon in an advertisement must be just as sincere as any other type of advertising copy. It cannot succeed by cleverness alone. It cannot copy the old-time irrelevant practice of the street corner medicine man, who sold nefarious concoctions by attracting a crowd with a blackface banjo player. (As a kid I used to see one of these "doctors" about once a month in my hometown of Bloomfield, Indiana, and I often think today how close some television programs come to being just old-fashioned banjo medicine shows.)

An advertising cartoon must not use the "switch." The first advertising cartoons were all wrong. They betrayed the confidence and injured the sensibilities of the reader by springing a gag which had nothing to do with the real motive of the advertisement they topped. A picture of a man being kicked over a fence by a mule somehow squirmed itself into becoming an advertisement for a jewelry store.

A humorous advertisement should admit right from the start that it is an advertisement. It should be honest from the top down, and this in itself can add to its magnetism. I agree with James D. Woolf of *Advertising Age*, when he says: "I am a strong believer in revealing *at once* what the copy is all about. . . . Trick headlines [or cartoons, say I] can have no purpose other than that of deceiving the reader, and I regard them as confessions of creative weakness on the part of the writers who perpetrate them."

I've never known exactly what my profession is—writer, advertising writer, layout man, typographer (I wrote a book on typography for the Advertising Typographers Association of America), photographer (I once wrote a book called *Enlarging is Thrilling*), golf pro (I'm a lousy golfer but once wrote a book called *Love That Golf*), doctor (see my book *The Happy Hypochondriac*), or cartoonist, but when somebody asks me what I am, I say *"cartoonist."*

I've learned that this is what interests them. They have little interest in any of my other so-called aptitudes.

As an earnest hypochondriac, I've spent no small part of my life in doctors' offices and hospitals. If I register as a cartoonist, I get class A1 attention. In hospitals the nurses swarm in to tell me about their little sons or nephews who want to be cartoonists, and they talk about their favorite cartoon strips. Yes, I'm sure everybody loves cartoonists, or at least cartoons.

I don't love all of them myself. It was Bud Fisher, I believe, who said, "Comic strip cartoonists don't make good husbands," to which I added, "And God knows they don't make good comic strips." For one thing, I have been sad to see so many comic strips become tragic strips in recent years.

In this book I have reproduced a number of good examples of the use of cartoons in advertising, and a few unfortunate flops.

I myself usually use advertising cartoons to lead into text or to make text seem more inviting.

I believe in text more than most cartoonists do, because I've tried cartoons both with and without text.

I'm convinced that a cartoon alone may be too flip. It may evoke the reaction, "That's cute," but it does not make a sale.

I myself do not draw people *as people* in my advertising cartoons, because people as people are, by and large, grotesque, even ugly.

I cannot abide the horrible creatures which have come into cartoons and into advertising in recent years in the name of modernity, with noses coming off the tops of foreheads, with two eyes on one side of the head, or with legs coming out of chins.

Since most of the characters we portray are representing either happy buyers of the product, or at least prospects, I believe we should not ask our readers to identify themselves with monsters.

That is why I usually use abstract drawings, almost diagrams or symbols, of people rather than real people—ovals, usually pleasant and smiling, so that no customer or prospect can possibly take offense. No bulbous noses or missing foreheads or retreating chins—just, usually, cherubic and (I hope) delightful suggestions of people.

My candidate for a good character of the very modern type, as used by many advertisers determined to be avant-garde.

I try, perhaps without too much strain, to give my cartoons an almost amateurish touch, because I feel this decreases the gap between my reader and myself, and because I remember the quote from Robert H. Isbell: "I suppose it requires, paradoxically, a super-professional to get up an advertisement without a trace of the professional touch."

This goes for lighthearted copy as well as for lighthearted cartoons.

↑↑

*"Nope, no course within a mile of here.
Someone must be playing a DOT!"*

Sure, the DOT's a legend for distance, but it's more. It's the truest putting golf ball ever made, features the toughest cover and finish ever put on any high-compression golf ball. *Only your golf professional sells the DOT.*

It's the DOT for distance

sets the pace in sports

As a rule, utterly impossible situations are not good in humorous advertising, but when a golf ball is the product, almost anything is all right, because of the endless kidding that goes with the game. So this far-fetched series on the Spalding Dot shoots par for the course. (Prepared for A. G. Spalding & Bros., Inc., by Young & Rubicam, Inc.; ARTIST: *Clarke*)

Golfers say it is incredible how the DOT cuts those back-breaking long holes down to size. Next time one looms up, tee up a DOT. Distance is its middle name.

DOTS can be personalized when you order a dozen or more. Sold through golf professionals only.

It's the DOT for distance

sets the pace in sports

Peanuts Characters © 1950 United Feature Syndicate, Inc.

FORD FALCON '62

BEST SHAPE ECONOMY'S EVER BEEN IN!

 This advertisement approved and the data certified true by United States Auto Club USAC

*With standard Falcon Six engine and manual transmission, driven in the cross-country test by an expert driver

A PRODUCT OF *Ford* MOTOR COMPANY

The sweet subtlety of Charles M. Schulz in his Peanuts advertising for the Falcon car, in both print and television, makes it one of the top cartoon advertising achievements of all time. Every advertising cartoonist in the business is envious of the success of Schulz in selling-with-humor in the Falcon campaign, handled by the J. Walter Thompson Company.

"Holy Smoke, you're salesmen—not jack rabbits!"

It didn't take the new sales manager long to diagnose the trouble. He soon demonstrated the weakness in his company's selling program.

A large wall map and a gross of red-headed pins were all he needed. With these he showed that the field men were forced to spend too much time traveling. Their territories straggled over too large an area.

Because Rand McNally Commercial Maps give home-office executives a simple, X-ray diagram of national and sectional markets, they have starred in many a sales reorganization program.

These Rand McNally Maps are edited from a business point of view . . . in many styles for many uses. Some are black and white; some are full color. Some have state lines only; some indicate the location of every place that has a name. Some are letterhead size; some will cover a mammoth wall.

Long recognized as the leading map-maker for the world, Rand McNally is becoming more and more the official map-maker for American business. You're invited to write for a catalog.

RAND McNALLY & COMPANY
Established 1856
NEW YORK · CHICAGO · SAN FRANCISCO · WASHINGTON · LOS ANGELES
School Books · School Maps · Children's Books · Road Maps
Travel Folders · Tickets · Coupon Books · Maps · Atlases
Globes · Bankers Monthly · Bankers Directory

I personally nominate Gluyas Williams as the best advertising cartoonist of all time. His characters always "sell" the proposition they are marketing, they are so genuine and so honest in emotional expressions, and his drawings are so capable and so clean that they bestow class on their subjects. Unfortunately, clips of Gluyas Williams cartoon ads seem to be so rare as to be almost museum pieces. Mr. Williams himself, with characteristic modesty, has not treasured and hoarded his own work. I wish I could reproduce a dozen of his masterpieces in this book. I am indebted to Henry J. Schilling, of Wakefield, N. Y., for digging up this rare old Williams for me.—*d.h.*

"But, Doctor, you can't leave now even if you do want to learn
the new steps at Arthur Murray's in time for the holidays."

Smart people will drop everything this week and rush to Arthur Murray's. . . . Why don't you? Make the hit of your life at holiday parties. Learning the new steps with our charming experts is grand fun. After only a few hours you'll have the Rumba or latest Fox Trot down pat. Arthur Murray. 11 East 43rd St. and 695 Fifth Ave. (54th St.)

The pleasant urgency of an appointment for a lesson at the Arthur Murray studios is humorously presented in this amusing ad. If you are "expecting," be sure your obstetrician is *not* a Murray pupil. (AGENCY: *Ruthrauff & Ryan [now Erwin Wasey, Ruthrauff & Ryan, Inc.]*)

"Ever notice how recess drags when you haven't
had your Wheaties?"

Bored? Listless? Disinterested? Drag yourself down to your grocer and get lots of milk, fruit, and Wheaties, "Breakfast of Champions." Zesty nourishment in those whole wheat flakes, exciting flavor. Wheaties put new life and **new** interest in your morning meal.

More cogent than a four-color portrait of a bowl of Wheaties is this small ad, one of a long-running newspaper series. One reason it is good is that it resembles a standard newspaper cartoon feature. (AGENCY: *Knox Reeves Advertising, Inc.*; CARTOONIST: Huffine)

Is Your Present Safe a Safe.....or a Stove?
By don herold

If that sounds like a silly question . . . well, don't go calling the crazy wagon for me just yet.

You can't exactly laugh off the fact that 43 out of 100 firms that lose their accounts receivable and other important business records in a fire *never reopen*.

A fire may cook your business goose

Most of those records get cremated in safes that act like stoves once an office fire gets above 350° F. (*Your* safe would probably act the same way—if it doesn't bear the Underwriters' Laboratories, Inc. label.)

Let me remind you, too, that a fire-proof building just hems in and heats up a fire that starts in an office. And another thing: your fire insurance policy says you have to produce a proof-of-loss statement in 60 days, to collect fully. There's not much chance for that, with ashes for records.

Why not check into a new Mosler Record Safe? Although it's the best, it doesn't cost anywhere near the fancy price most people think.

MODEL 4216CL—New "100" Series Mosler Record Safe. Dimensions overall: 52" high x 22" wide x 24" deep. F.O.B. Mosler Store, **only $298**

IF IT'S MOSLER...IT'S SAFE

The Mosler Safe Company
Since 1848

World's Largest Builders of Safes and Bank Vaults

This "DANGERater" is a fire risk "exposure meter"

It's *FREE*, too! Mail coupon for yours, today. Accurate. Authentic. Based on experience with thousands of fires. Dials your exact risk in 30 seconds. Tells whether your records are really protected!

THE MOSLER SAFE COMPANY
(Branch Address)

Please send free Mosler Fire "DANGERater" and new illustrated catalog of all Mosler Record Safes.

NAME...

ADDRESS...

CITY..

ZONE...........STATE.............................

Cartoons can sometimes dramatize a truth which a photo would present blah-ly. This one, with a startling headline, conveys its message more sellingly than a photograph of a burning office. (AGENCY: *Stockton, West, Burkhart, Inc.*)

69

MORAL: When you need an Indian costume for a fancy dress ball, or three dozen cake plates for a church supper, or a second-hand bulldozer for a lawn party—you'll find anything and everything in the Yellow Pages of your telephone directory. Follow General Custer's brave example—use your Yellow Pages often. *Let your fingers do the walking!*

One of a really amusing cartoon series in comic sections for the Yellow Pages, for Pacific Northwest Bell. Another shows George Washington's staff looking up "Barges," "Boats," "Dinghies," on the banks of the Delaware. (AGENCY: *Guild, Bascom & Bonfigli, Inc.*)

H. T. Webster was often called the Mark Twain of cartoonists. His true ear for family dialogue made him a fine man to use to make potent points for any product used in the home. (*From the archives of Henry J. Schilling*)

Surprise is frequently a sure-fire element in humorous advertising. This ad is crazy enough to have terrific appeal and is much more effective, I think, than the later Pepsi-Cola theme, "For those who think young," which, it seems to me, appeals only to octogenarians who think they think young. (CARTOONIST: *O.Soglow*)

How thin is THIN?

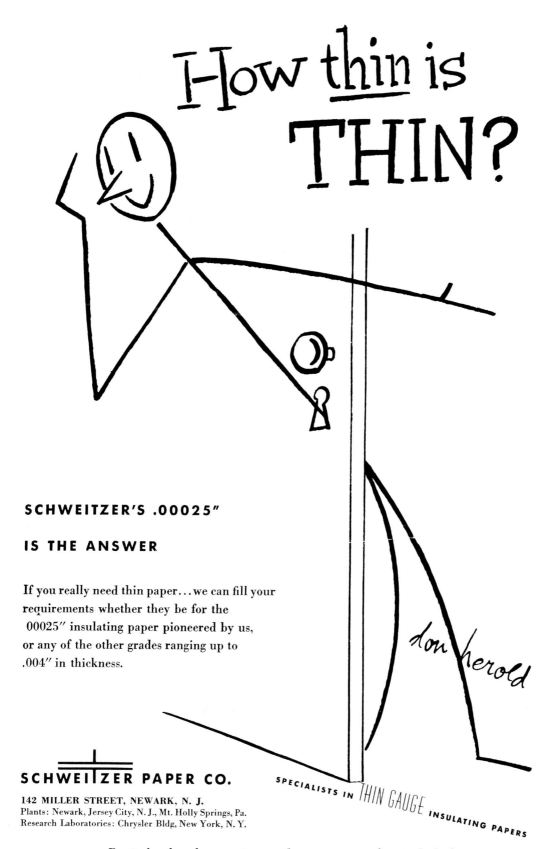

SCHWEITZER'S .00025"

IS THE ANSWER

If you really need thin paper...we can fill your requirements whether they be for the 00025" insulating paper pioneered by us, or any of the other grades ranging up to .004" in thickness.

don herold

SCHWEITZER PAPER CO.

142 MILLER STREET, NEWARK, N. J.
Plants: Newark, Jersey City, N. J., Mt. Holly Springs, Pa.
Research Laboratories: Chrysler Bldg, New York, N. Y.

SPECIALISTS IN *THIN GAUGE* INSULATING PAPERS

Pretty hard to draw a picture of paper .00025 of an inch thick, so I used symbolism here, for the Schweitzer Paper Company in these trade-paper ads for their extremely thin insulating paper. —*d.h.*

talk about absorbency

As a result of considerable research, we have developed grades of electrolytic condenser paper which have outstanding qualities of absorbency and purity. This is in addition to the uniformity characteristic of our other grades of thin gauge insulating papers ranging in thickness from .00025″ to .004″.

SCHWEITZER PAPER CO.

142 MILLER STREET, NEWARK, N. J.
Plants: Newark, Jersey City, Mt. Holly Springs, Pa. Research Laboratories: Chrysler Bldg., New York, N. Y.

SPECIALISTS IN THIN GAUGE INSULATING PAPERS

And a cartoon interpretation of the absorbency of electrolytic condenser paper, in another trade-paper ad for another product of the Schweitzer Paper Company. —d.h.

Though this ad for Guiness was originally published more than 20 years ago, it is remembered by us as one of the happiest cartoon ads of all time. (Cartoon by Fougasse, famous *Punch* artist. AGENCY: *S. H. Benson Ltd., London,* whose letterhead describes them refreshingly as "Incorporated Practitioners in Advertising.")

"I feel like a Guinness."
"I wish you were."

Most telephone advertising does not say "Install a telephone," but rather, "Call up Grandma." Here's a merry variation from the "loved ones" theme, as offered by Northwestern Bell. They won't get rich from calls placed by customers who have bagged a moose (is that a moose?) but the series is so gay, that we're sure it will set a lot of phones tingling. (AGENCY: *Batten, Barton, Durstine & Osborn, Inc., Minneapolis;* ARTIST: *Lowell Herrero*)

GOT NEWS TO SHARE?

Pick up the phone and delight your faraway friends and relatives with a friendly call—they're always interested in the latest happenings at your house. *Save time...call by number Save money...call station-to-station.*

Northwestern Bell in Nebraska

"What! No Kitchen Telephone?"

Another bell ringer for Bell Telephone, national. Even though she is being carried across all the thresholds, this bride notes in horror that there's no phone in the kitchen, and is evidently wasting no time in raising Cain about it.

Of all things, Mr. Bridegroom! Surely you don't expect that lovely new bride to get along without a telephone in the kitchen!

Maybe there was a time when one telephone seemed enough. But everybody is used to more comfort and convenience these days. And there's nothing that makes life so much easier as telephones around the home.

In the living room, of course. In the kitchen, conveniently hung on the wall. In the bedroom, to save steps and for added peace of mind both day and night.

Would you like to know more about complete telephone service and how surprisingly little it costs? Just call the business office of your local Bell telephone company.

BELL TELEPHONE SYSTEM

Any cord-tangled family can
live a better life with PLUGMOLD,
the surface wiring system that puts
outlets where you want them and
feeds *full power to each outlet.* Not
just another kind of extension cord,
all-steel PLUGMOLD offers a variety of outlet spacing and wiring
capacities, goes neatly in *any* building. PLUGMOLD GIVES MORE
OUTLETS FOR LESS MONEY.
Write The Wiremold Company,
Hartford 10, Conn. for full data.

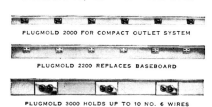

PLUGMOLD 2000 FOR COMPACT OUTLET SYSTEM

PLUGMOLD 2200 REPLACES BASEBOARD

PLUGMOLD 3000 HOLDS UP TO 10 NO. 6 WIRES

PLUGMOLD BY
WIREMOLD®

"Listen, Doc, I'd rather be home
reading John Roy Carlson's swell
comic-strip, 'Underground', in the
Herald Tribune. I gotta find out
what happened when Jim dropped
that atomic heat-ray machine!"
*You're missing plenty if you
don't read the Herald Tribune
—N.Y.'s most interesting paper.*

Cartoons Make Small Space Ads Stand Out

If you'll whisk though any publication you'll note that the
ads that catch your eye are usually those with cartoons—even
though the ads may be quite small. This is because of your
continuous hunger for amusement and your eternal interest
in the unconventional. Cartoons are definitely *stoppers,* and
are therefore of great economical service wherever they may
be legitimately used.

Tiny cartoons can snag the eye and often get attention equal to that won by conventional ads ten times as big.

If you light your first Rocky Ford before you reach for your change, don't make the old mistake of trying to give the clerk back a nickel! He'll just slide it back to you with a grin. . . . 'cause nearly every day some appreciative cigar smoker tries to pay a dime for a Rocky Ford. It does taste like a ten center. . . . . but it costs only a nickel!

ROCKY FORD is long-filler, Sumatra wrapped. Made in a sunlit factory, the pride and show-factory of Richmond, Virginia . . . a factory as clean as a modern bakery . . . a factory that is automatic machine-equipped throughout.

the better

5¢ cigar

Rocky Ford

"where's my Honey?"

Right here . . . golden-hued Golden Blossom! Ready to add luscious natural sweetness to your pancakes, toast, spreads. Honey soothes your throat . . . gives you quick energy through its wholesome, easily digestible sugars. For flavor, for health . . . no wonder everybody asks "Where's my honey?" Here, yes . . . but sorry, not yet in quantity.

here!

GOLDEN BLOSSOM BRAND HONEY

READING DICK TRACY?   NO, LOOKING AT A SMALL AD.

Cartoons and lettering on left by F. G. Cooper

Cartoon on right by Virgil Partch

THERE'S AN EASIER WAY TO GET EXTRA
CASH

Vip

SEE COMMERCIAL CREDIT PLAN

Why do it the hard way? Call on the Commercial Credit Plan* whenever you can use extra cash. Our loan service is fast, friendly and convenient. Rates are reasonable. That's why thousands of families prefer to use Commercial Credit Plan* It's the pay *way* that fits your pay *day!* Keep this ad as a reminder to phone or visit us.

HOW MUCH DO YOU NEED?			
Cash You Get	Monthly Payments For		
	24 Mo.	18 Mo.	12 Mo.
$200	$ 9.37	$12.16	$17.75
300	14.06	18.24	26.62
500	23.43	30.41	44.37
750	35.15	45.62	66.56
1000	46.87	60.83	88.75
1250	58.60	76.04	110.94

* A service offered by
COMMERCIAL CREDIT
CORPORATION

7 West St.
Phone: PI 8-5681

When the mortgage is right everything looks bright!

It's wonderful how the right kind of mortgage loan can improve your feelings towards your house and towards life in general.

Yes, your mortgage loan is very important, because you are going to live with it closely for 15 or 29 years or more.

Give it a lot of thought, and let ARONOVITCH & LEIPSIC LIMITED, mortgage specialists, give it a lot of thought, too. Their mortgage loan will be easy to live with.

Even though your home may be just a dream now, plan to go to ARONOVITCH & LEIPSIC LIMITED for "the mortgage loan in your future."

A & L Bldg.
Four Sixty Main Ph. WH 2-3301

SMALL ADS
IN THE OBSERVER

A LITTLE PACKAGE WITH A BIG BANG

"It feels good up here"

You're sitting on top of the world if you've saved money here. You have a secure —even a slightly saucy and superior—feeling. How to save? Bring the first $5 or $10 to us and leave it and add every possible penny when you can.

RED BANK SAVINGS AND LOAN ASSOCIATION
10 Broad Street
Red Bank, New Jersey
Chartered 1887

Monday thru Friday
Open 9 a. m. to 4 p. m.

Tel. SHadyside 7-0330

Accounts Insured to $10,000

They don't sell insurance— they BUY it for you

We study your insurance needs and buy your policy for you of the company which can insure you best and most reasonably.

Stockton, Whatley, Davin & Company

Mortgages — Insurance
573 - First Avenue North
Telephone 7-3631

Does humor pay off? The Ford cartoon ad on the left scored better than the more serious ad on the right, in a survey made by Daniel Starch & Staff: MEN: *Noted:* 42 to 32; *Read most:* 20 to 5. WOMEN: *Noted:* 28 to 14; *Read most:* 13 to 1. Both ads appeared as full pages in *Life.* Comparison published in *Printers' Ink.* (AGENCY: *J. Walter Thompson Company, Detroit*)

Expansion Joint Design Moves out of the "Model T" Era

Badger first began fabricating packless metal bellows expansion joints more than 35 years ago. These "Model T" joints performed (and are still performing) with outstanding success in hundreds of process and steam line piping installations.

Starting in the 30's other expansion joint manufacturers entered the field. The most successful adopted many of the basic features of the original Badger design.

During the last decade, as industry's requirements became more stringent, and joint manufacturers gained fabricating and field experience, certain fundamental problems inherent in the early designs became evident. Most of these problems were solved through a series of modifications. (Among which was the Badger Directed Flexing Self-Equalizing Joint — the famous "DFSE" Design.) But, at best, the modifications were stop-gap measures which complicated the joints and greatly increased their weight. A fundamental reassessment of expansion joint engineering data was needed. Badger led the way: In 1956, a task force completed a three-year research program and the first S-R (Service-Rated) Expansion Joints were produced.

In the three years they have been available, S-R Expansion Joints have been both an engineering and a sales success. But like many revolutionary concepts which upset tradition, the full implication of the advantages S-R Joints offer is still not universally understood. The message that follows is an attempt "to set the record straight."

· · · · ·

Equalization — fact and fiction

Many users of expansion joints are under the impression that the so-called "equalizing" rings on today's conventional type expansion joints distribute movement equally among all the corrugations of the bellows. It is argued that as the joint absorbs thermal movement, the tops of the rings progressively come into contact until the bellows is fully compressed thus limiting the amount of compression which any one corrugation can ultimately absorb (see diagram 1). In this sense the rings do contribute to the "equalization" of movement by physically limiting the compression of each corrugation to the distance between any two adjacent rings.

Conventional Type Expansion Joint. Cross-sections of rings and bellows of a conventional "self-equalizing" joint showing cold and hot positions. Note that true equalization of movement can only be obtained when tops of all rings are in contact — an impractical and dangerous situation.

Note, however, that the degree of compression will not be truly equalized until the tops of all the rings are in contact. But, when such a condition occurs, serious problems will result. If the limit of compressibility is reached before the thermal expansion has been completely absorbed, exceedingly large forces will be transmitted through the pipe line to the anchors and connected equipment. On the other hand, if the joint is compressed only partially, not all of the corrugations will absorb movement to the same degree.

How S-R Joints solve equalization problem

Badger S-R Expansion Joints feature the new Curvilinear Corrugations which naturally assume an "all curve" shape under pressure (diagram 2), assuring more equal distribution of stresses throughout the bellows material. Furthermore, the shape, height and pitch of the corrugations are based on a carefully engineered correlation. Thus, reasonably equal distribution of movement among the corrugations is obtained, even in joints not equipped with reinforcing rings.

Badger S-R Expansion Joint. Cross-sections of S-R Joints (Series 50 left, Series 150 right). The movement of the corrugations is shown by dotted and solid lines. Compare configuration and effective height of corrugation, position and size of rings with conventional joint.

Equalization of movement is inherent in the design and functioning of the bellows on Badger S-R Joints. On the basis of provable engineering criteria, the prime purpose of reinforcing rings of any design is to retain the hoop dimension (diameter) of the corrugations when they are subject to internal pressure. This Badger's simple, lightweight tubular reinforcing rings do. But, in addition, the new tubular shape of the rings does contribute to joint flexibility and life by permitting flexing over a more effective portion of the total corrugation height than conventional cast or fabricated equalizing rings.

Better performance, lower cost

Briefly, then, Badger S-R Joints alone offer these advantages: Better equalization of movement which results in elimination of localized stresses and leads to longer joint life; a simple, lightweight design that makes installation easier, eliminates cumbersome castings and fragile mechanical devices; complete range of sizes from 3" to 72" made from any workable metal and with a wide choice of accessories.

Badger S-R Joints are probably the answer to your problem. There's an easy and quick way to find out — ask the Badgerman for his recommendations. Write or phone today. Badger Manufacturing Co., 230 Bent St., Cambridge, Mass.

BADGER S·R EXPANSION JOINTS

© COPYRIGHT 1959 BADGER MFG. CO.

HOW TO SLEUTH OUT THE TRUTH ABOUT EXPANSION JOINTS

1 Case the joint (design, that is)
Badger S-R Expansion Joints have: 1. Corrugations which assume "all curve" shape under pressure for low stress, long life. 2. Tubular rings allow flexing over more of corrugation height.

2 "Weigh" the evidence
S-R Joints have no bulky castings . . . weigh up to 50% less . . . diameter equivalent to pipe flange. Installation is easier, lighter supports required.

3 Search for clues in fabrication methods
Bellows are hydraulically formed to produce uniform corrugations with minimum thinning of material. Quality controlled longitudinal welding, no multiple circumferential welds.

4 Remember to look for accessories
Full line of accessories — including covers and liners. Easy to pick proper combination of model, type and accessories for any pressure, temperature, erosive or corrosive condition.

5 Pull an M.O. on the manufacturer's background
Badger's 50-year experience includes development of first successful self-equalizing design for higher pressures, temperatures. Badger has had more fabrication and engineering experience in more different applications than any other manufacturer.

6 Close the case — buzz Badger
See the Badgerman for expert help on your most exacting pipe expansion problems. He knows his business, your problems. Call or write today.

Badger S·R
Expansion Joints
BADGER MANUFACTURING COMPANY
230 Bent Street, Cambridge 41, Mass.
Representatives in Principal Cities

© 1960 BMC

Humor (cartoons) versus solemnity. Of the above ads for the Badger Company, Inc. (formerly Badger Manufacturing Company), the one on the left scored better against the more serious ad on the right, in a survey made by Daniel Starch & Staff. Comparison published in *Printers' Ink*. MEN: *Noted:* 26 to 10; *Read most:* 10 to 4. Both ads appeared in *Power* magazine. (AGENCY: *F. P. Walther, Jr. and Associates, Inc., Boston*)

Humor Gets Long Copy Read

There are no dull stories—there are just dull story tellers.

—GEORGE HORACE LORIMER

Brevity as brevity has had a lot of blind acclaim from maxim-minded advertising novitiates.

Length, as length, has taken a lot of unjust raps.

I'll agree that any message that seems long is too long. Any boresome message is too long. (Some people can write two-line letters that are too long.)

Every line of advertising that is written has a double function to perform. Each paragraph must not only partially sell the product, but it must also sell the next paragraph. Anybody who can bring this off can produce a message as long as Katherine Anne Porter's *Ship of Fools* and still hold readers and sell merchandise.

A good percentage of advertising messages I read don't tell me half enough. Too many of them attempt to be cute and quick. If the topic is of any fundamental interest to me, I want all there is to know about it.

As a writer, I never *intend* to write more than one paragraph about anything. Thank God I am as lazy as hell, and I want to do every job the shortest way. If I write more than one paragraph, it's because I simply can't help myself. I get excited. I let the writing write me. I get so sold on the product I'm selling that I can't quit. And maybe I convey some of this zeal to my readers.

Let's admit that there are more ads demanding attention today and more products calling for consideration, and that there may sometimes be great justification for merely opening the prospect's door and yelling *"Boo!"*

But let's remember that longer copy undeniably brings home the bacon, if you can get people to read it.

Certainly, you would like to get everybody possible to listen to your story a full half hour if you could get away with it and succeed in winning rapt attention.

That's lots better always than a lick and a promise.

Today there is a veritable plethora of magazine ads with the top three-quarters of the page devoted to an illustration and the bottom quarter or less devoted to a few scant lines of copy.

The effect is a monotonous sameness in ad formats, a reticence in copy that almost seems to be a reluctance to discuss the product, and sometimes even gives an impression of apology. And many times out of ten the effect is glibness, and often a smart-aleck pseudosophisticated brush-off.

It's funny how herd-minded advertisers are. Where individuality can count for so much, we have eras of slavish conformity to prevalent momentary practices. For, say, ten years, almost the whole profession will go in droves in one direction.

Lots of ads today—thousands of them—are *nothing but short.*

The first thing any young new advertising manager learns to say today is: "Make the copy shorter." He regards this as evidence of his arrival at hard-boiled professionalism.

But if you have a job to do, there is no sense in doing a useless fifth of it, *just to be brief.*

When someone asked Abraham Lincoln how long a man's legs should be, he replied, "Long enough to reach to the ground."

Displaying a decided improvement in the vigor of his advertising copy, a young writer, when asked how it came about, replied: "I'm writing each advertisement as if it is the only one which will appear this year on that product."

Right here, maybe we are getting at one of the main reasons for using humor in advertising copy.

Each paragraph sells the next paragraph, because it leads the reader on, and pays him, in entertainment, for his time.

Instead of giving your reader twelve or fifty-two scattered installment doses of your story, give him as much of the complete story as you can get away with, and if humor will help you do it, and the subject lends itself to light treatment, use humor.

How do you know any reader is going to see every one of twelve ads in a scattered series of twelve? The cumulative effect you see on the bulletin board in your office is certainly never

going to be achieved "in the field." Maybe your prospect is going to see only one, two, or three of your series. So maybe you'd better tell him the whole works, once you have him buttonholed.

William Randolph Hearst said he wrote long editorials because the uninterested reader could

always quit at any point, whereas the interested reader could read on and find enough to satisfy him.

It's a cinch that people who *have* to make sales in print, no fooling, usually use long copy—for instance, the patent medicine people. They don't depend on quickie messages or mere flashes.

Pa Kavenew has said:

Words bring coupons! We may wish we could bring in a bucketful of responses with a short, gay epigram and a brief, allusive burst of copy, but when we pack a client's space with clear, reasonable and credible reasons why the reader should respond, "long copy" again proves its uncanny ability to catch the fish.

However, "reasons why" are not enough nowadays, unless they are presented with charm and lightness.

Of course, either overdone brevity or overdone length can be the result of laziness on the part of the creative man.

It's mighty easy to leave the top three-quarters of an ad to an artist or to a photographer. You can always tell the art director or artist or photographer to submit twelve, and try again. And it's easier to plan a campaign of twelve or fifty-two ads repeating a single idea, than it is to write twelve or fifty-two fascinating pieces of copy. It's easier to get short ads up in a bunch in advance to submit to the client, and it's easier on the client to ask him to okay quickies than to study longies. But there's usually so much money involved in space cost that laziness and expediency should never enter into the choice of techniques.

However, the laziness which results in long-windedness was commented on humorously by Joseph Pulitzer. In closing a long letter to an aide, he wrote: "Pardon the length of this letter; I haven't time to write a short one."

It takes more time to write lively complete copy than to write dull short copy, but if the effort wins two to five times as many "long readers," the cost is well worthwhile.

Pictures are a lazier way out for agency executives than good copy, and are often sold to the client with the old adage, "One picture is worth, etc. . . ."

Richard Powell (not the late TV producer) said in *Publishers' Weekly*: "One of the most ridiculous statements ever made is that one picture is worth a thousand words. As an example, I give you not a thousand words but eleven words, and I ask you to put across their message in a picture: 'Do unto others as you would have others do unto you.'"

It took heavenly inspiration and a lot of time to produce those eleven words.

Someone else remarked that if one picture is worth a thousand words, why didn't the author of this epigram use a picture to say it?

But even these eleven wonderful words did not make a complete Bible. It took several hundred well-written biblical pages to put the full Message across.

Don Francisco, a skilled old-timer in advertising, once wrote:

Mail-order advertisers, who can check the results from every advertisement they run, usually find that long copy is most profitable. They find it is better to have twenty people read the entire advertisement and be convinced than to have 100 people merely see it.

Most advertising does not say enough. The best advertising is that which is informative and renders a service to the reader.

Fred Decker, publisher of *Printers' Ink*, in lamenting today's vogue of exaggerated brevity of copy, said:

I particularly have in mind a magazine that very much wants to increase its share of market, but which is spending a small fortune on art that bleeds across two pages and is accompanied by only a one-line slogan, ad after ad.

I wish this publisher, and a number of others, would regain their appreciation of the power of the written word to inform, inspire, and motivate. I wish he would reduce the art in his advertising, and sharply increase the length and informativeness of his copy. If he would, I am sure he would get far more advertising value per dollar expended.

In The Creative Man's Corner in *Advertising Age*, I find the following: "So many ads these days are skillfully done in the art area but so woefully weak when it comes to copy. Maybe before too long copy will catch up to the mighty strides advertising design has made."

Short copy can often result in a breakdown in communications, and this is one of the great evils of the rush of modern life. We just don't take the time or trouble to *explain*, often even in our ads.

I just want to stand up and combat the automatic copybook maxim that you get thrown at you perennially: Keep it short. Of course, keep it short. Suffer to keep it short. But if the message and your passion for completing it call for length, give it length.

For, one thing, you'll look different and *be* different from 95 per cent of the advertising in publications today.

And if you want to get length, use humor to make the length seem shorter.

In adjoining pages, I am showing examples of "long-copy" ads, readable and effective, I believe, because they were written lightly.

6⅞"

YES IT IS RATHER ODD FOR A TEA COMPANY TO MENTION THE WORD COFFEE IN AN AD

Many of the people who have written to enter Salada's Coffee Bean Guessing Bee have allowed as how it was a bit eccentric for us to go around saying coffee in broad daylight. As a matter of fact it is, but who are we kidding by hushing it up? Let's lay our leaves on the table. There are other things to drink besides tea, and if you don't know it, we'd rather you found it out from us. 🍃 We go on the theory that if you bring a subject like coffee right out into the open, people will be less curious about it and eventually lose interest in it. That's why you will never catch us vaguely referring to the other side as "Brand X" or possibly: "the expensive brew." It's called <u>coffee</u>. That's its name. 🍃 Having dispensed with that let us get down to more important matters. This being Salada's Seventieth Year in the tea game, we are currently sponsoring a contest to guess how many coffee beans are contained in the glass tea canister pictured at left and the entries are pouring in. If you haven't

(CONTINUED IN LOWER LEFT HAND BOX)

(CONTINUED FROM UPPER RIGHT HAND BOX)

done so yet, you may still participate in the bee by clipping the coupon. 🍃 Remember the closest guess wins the beautiful sterling tea service, a year's supply of Salada Tea, the tea canister and the coffee beans. If you've watched television lately you know what fun they're having with coffee beans. Running their fingers through them and all that. Five years ago it was hula hoops...this year it's coffee beans. 🍃 After playing with the beans, fill your canister with Salada and prepare yourself for the most terrific cup of tea you'll ever taste. After 70 years we've sort of got it down to a fine point. 🍃 At any rate don't lose any sleep on our account worrying about the use of the word coffee in our ads. All it can do is get Salada Tea in a lot of hot water. We certainly hope so.

The Salada Tea Co., Woburn, Mass.

Sirs: I'm sorry I haven't gotten around to entering your coffee bean guessing bee yet, but I've been out of town. I'd say there are _____ beans in the tea canister. If I win, send along my sterling silver tea service, my year's supply of Salada Tea, my tea canister and my coffee beans. I prefer bags ( ), bulk ( ). I understand the beans have been counted and are being held by BRINKS INC., and that the winner will be announced in a forthcoming ad. You sound like a game tea company.

My name is _____

My address is _____

Nobody but uninhibited and unlimited Freberg, Ltd., would use coffee beans in a contest in a group of ads to sell tea (Salada). But Stan Freberg did it so joyously in this happy series for Salada that the first two drew 22,000 entries. (Photographer: *Max Yavno.*) A radio series running at the same time purported to be coffee commercials but did a gladsome job of selling Salada Tea. Quote: "A good substitute for people who can't afford psychoanalysis—a nice calming cup of soothing Salada Tea."

Gentlemen Know When to Quit
by don herold

Maybe I'm something of an expert on moderation, especially since I wrote that book—"Drunks Are Driving Me To Drink."

So (naturally) I thought that the Stitzel-Weller people were smart when they came and asked me to write a campaign for them on moderation. These people own the fine, old-family distillery that makes OLD CABIN STILL Bourbon in Louisville.

They say they don't like excessive drinkers any more than I do. For one thing, they have only a small distillery, and they don't want anybody to try to drink them out of business.

They are making OLD CABIN STILL to appeal especially to sportsmen (and to sportsman-like drinkers) and I really believe sportsmen will like this bourbon because it has a rich, substantial, outdoor flavor. (You can really taste it, so you don't have to drink a lot of it to enjoy it.)

Every drop of it is distilled, aged and bottled only by Stitzel-Weller in the same slow, patient, costly, sour-mash way the family has been using for generations.

These folks would no more put any but their own bourbon into an OLD CABIN STILL bottle, than a good sportsman would *buy* a fish at the A & P and claim he caught it, himself.

You can do too much of anything—eat too much, fish too much, work too hard, or take too much medicine. I think these OLD CABIN STILL people are forthright and foresighted to come out—gentlemen distillers that they are—and make an appeal for gentlemanly moderation in the use of their rather rare product.

OLD CABIN STILL
The Sportsman's Choice!

Kentucky Straight Bourbon. Balanced at the Flavor Proof—91. Distilled, aged and bottled only by Stitzel-Weller Distillery, Estab. Louisville, Ky., 1849.

Conservation through Moderation... with gun, rod or bottle.

Shortly after I wrote a series of "temperate drinking" ads for Old Cabin Still bourbon in national magazines, their agency, Winius Brandon Company, of St. Louis, wrote me: "Our Starches on your columns show as high 'read most' as full-pages in four colors, which is gratifying, especially considering your copy ran about 300 words as compared to the scant body copy in the garden-variety of product display ads." —*d.h.*

YOU'RE TALKING IN A SOUND-PROOF ROOM

by don herold

You're talking strictly sub-rosa when you discuss your dream of a new plant with a man from the Industrial Development (plant location) Staff of the B&O Railroad.

He knows your plans are none of your competitors' business.

He knows you have to pick up the real estate before it gets expensive because-you-want-it.

He knows you probably desire iron-curtain secrecy for your plans—no matter how embryonic they are at this stage.

You'll find it is part of his professional ethics to keep as mum as a Baltimore oyster.

What you want is a location where you have the economic atmosphere essential to profitable production. Location alone can often mean the difference between a nice profit and serious loss. Other elements which the B&O man can help you appraise dollar-and-cents wise are: POWER, WATER, LABOR, FUEL, SITES, TRANSPORTATION, TAXES, MARKETS, WEATHER, RAW MATERIALS and your own peculiar problem.

The B&O says "*Ask our man.*" Write or phone for one of the B&O's Industrial Development men at:

New York 4	Phone: DIgby	4-1600
Baltimore 1	Phone: LExington	0400
Pittsburgh 22	Phone: COurt	1-6220
Cincinnati 2	Phone: DUnbar	2900
Chicago 7	Phone: WAbash	2-2211

They'll provide comprehensive plant location surveys without cost to you.

The heart of America's markets and the treasureland of the "lion's share" of America's industrial resources.

BALTIMORE & OHIO RAILROAD

Constantly *doing things—* **better!**

Here's a theme that couldn't possibly be put over in short copy. The answer is a curiosity-arousing cartoon and an intriguing headline with, I believe, compelling interest for anybody thinking of moving his factory to a new location or of building a new one somewhere, plus a strong argument or two for consulting the B. & O. plant-location department. —*d.h.* (AGENCY: *The Richard A. Foley Advertising Agency, Inc. [now Bayer, Trip-Foley, Inc.]*)

What idiot changed the Chivas Regal bottle?

When the Chivas Regal people changed their bottle recently, they were ready for some protests.

Not a storm of outrage.

At first, it does seem outrageous.

Why change a classic bottle?

A magnificent dark green bottle. And an antique shield that seemed to come out of Sir Walter Scott.

"It's a wonder they kept the shape," muttered one Chivas Regal fan.

True, the shape is the same.

Still squat. Still jaunty.

Most important, the Scotch inside is still the same Chivas Regal.

Not a day younger than 12 years. "Goode olde whiskie is a

Old.

heavenly spirit."

Then why change the bottle to clear flint glass? Why lighten the antique shield?

Because we live in an age of confusions.

One minor confusion is "light" Scotch.

People think of "light" Scotch

New.

as light in color. Color has nothing to do with "lightness."

People think of "light" Scotch as "weakened" whisky. Not so. Almost all Scotch is the same 86 proof.

True lightness is actually the "smoothness" of Scotch.

A light Scotch will go down as easily as water. Or honey.

No "back bite." No gasp. No wince. No shudder.

Many people consider Chivas Regal the smoothest (or lightest) Scotch in the world.

Why?

Since 1786, Chivas Regal has been made with the "soft" Highland Scotch of Glenlivet. (This is prize Scotch whisky.)

Extravagant sherry casks are still brought from Spain for ripening it. (Each costs over £35.)

Chivas Regal is still the same clear gold color it has always been.

This color is what warrants changing the bottle.

Many people have never tasted Chivas Regal, because its clear golden color never showed.

Handsome though it was, the old dark green bottle made Chivas Regal look dark.

Some people translated this as "heavy."

Many people never saw Chivas Regal in a restaurant or bar.

The old dark bottle and label almost hid it.

Same great Scotch inside.

No longer.

The new clear bottle offers an uninterrupted view of Chivas Regal.

And a warm welcome.

Think of it that way, and it's not so idiotic, is it?

It's kind of brilliant.

12-YEAR-OLD BLENDED SCOTCH WHISKY. 86 PROOF. GENERAL WINE AND SPIRITS CO., N.Y., N.Y.

Any dedicated Scotch drinker will have enough self-interest to read every word of this gaily written Chivas Regal ad. And he will finish with a compelling desire to try Chivas Regal. The light-vein copy, the short paragraphs, and the simple, inviting typography will help attract and hold valuable readers to the very end. (AGENCY: *Doyle Dane Bernbach Inc.*)

Copy that is a little longer than usual gets itself read because of the zany headline, the cartoons, and the appeal to the natural interest and curiosity of any businessman with money, valuable papers, or a shirt to put in a safe. The middle cartoon helps sell surprising reasonableness of price. (AGENCY: *Stockton, West, Burkhart, Inc.*)

Worry is a science
I LET EXPERTS DO MINE
by don herold

I HATE WORRY—

I know that it's no good for me.

So I send a lot of my worrying out . . . like laundry.

When you or I accumulate a family, a house, a car, furniture, jewelry and things, we find we also accumulate a flock of worries about risks accidents, and liabilities.

Disasters *can* happen, and if we've any sense we worry about their happening. But if we've still more sense, we pay a modest fee to specialists to do the worrying for us. I mean insurance companies — for instance AMERICA FORE — who are large-scale or mass-production worriers and can therefore do worrying at economical rates.

Insurance is about the most civilized achievement of mankind. When everything else breaks down, insurance stands up; *that* is its business. It is a device by which a lot of us can chip in a small amount to a large pool,

and the losers are the winners.

I think I have a lot better use for my 'brain than to worry—for example —if lightning is going to strike my house . . . or if Mrs. Herold is going to run over somebody with our station wagon . . . or if I'm going to break a leg . . . or if the milkman is going to sue me for tripping on our portico . . . or if Junior is going to hit somebody with a baseball . . .

At surprisingly moderate cost, I've delegated all such stewing . . . and other troubles . . . to the local representative of AMERICA FORE—a group of big, strong insurance companies who take practically every known everyday risk for you.

NEW INSURANCE WRINKLES

I've dug into insurance pretty thoroughly lately and I find that I haven't known beans about improvements and combinations made in insurance coverages in recent years—yes, months.

When the automobile companies bring out new models, you can see them in show windows. But when an insurance company brings out new models they're sorta invisible to the masses.

SO I'VE WRITTEN A BOOKLET

I got so fascinated with this subject that I've gone and written a booklet about it in the form of a QUIZ, to help the average man learn about new insurance wrinkles and to size up his coverages.

I've called this new booklet of mine "YOUR INSURANCE QUIZ—a *Question and Answer Game—for Fun—and Maybe Money.*"

You may have a free copy if you'll ask the America Fore representative in your vicinity or if you'll mail the nearby coupon today.

Signed ads, while not always advisable, have several advantages. They have a testimonial value, and they permit informality of writing often impossible over or under a sedate corporate signature. They can also allow the conveying of a sincere personal experience that may sound more convincing than a lot of abstract, presumptuous "you" talk. The reader easily imagines himself in the writer's shoes. (AGENCY: *Prince & Company, Inc.*)

-AND GOLF CARS ADD TO IT FOR ALL GOLFERS

So, love that golf car—and keep on lovin' that golf course too!

BY DON HEROLD,
Author of "Love That Golf"

I say, golf is 20% for exercise and 80% for pleasure.

So, I maintain that golf cars fill a long-felt need in bringing more pleasure to the game. They are not only here to stay, but almost daily, fleets of cars are being added to courses all over the country.

They'll add to golf pleasure for a larger and larger percentage of club members and greens fee patrons, just as improved courses, improved clubs, improved grasses and improved mowers and other improved equipment have all added to golf pleasure. And, they'll add greatly to club income.

I use cars a lot, and I love 'em. And —

GOLF CARS CALL FOR NEW RESPECT FOR THE COURSE

Since most of us are going to use cars, we must be sure we use them for the good of the course.

Most golf course superintendents have accepted golf cars open-heartedly, after seeing how much they add to the pleasure of many golfers and how they add to the profit of the club. At first, the superintendents were afraid cars would injure the turf, but this fear has been dispelled.

I think golf course superintendents are great people — they're the men really behind our golfing pleasure — and I think we should cooperate with them in every way.

Here are some suggestions I have gleaned from interviews with a number of them:

This Worthington CHAMP rides like a dream

It will add 15 years to my golfing life

B-110

1. Let your golf course superintendent be the judge of when turf conditions permit the use of cars on the course.
2. Keep your car 30 feet from greens.
3. Stay 30 feet away from water pockets.
4. Stay off tees.
5. Don't drive in areas between sand bunkers and greens.
6. Don't overload. No hitch-hikers. Two players and two bags to a car.

Cartoons and lively photos and a generous portion of "public service" copy on use of golf carts with consideration for golf courses, makes this long copy readable, and it brought in many requests for reprints for posting on club bulletin boards. (AGENCY: *Richard La Fond Advertising, Inc.*)

Where will we play today?

Let's go to Bonnie Wee. They have golf cars. I quit 5 years ago, but now I can play again - with a car - and a full 18 holes - and I've never enjoyed golf so much.

7. Don't be a "hot-rodder." Don't "horse around." Your car is not a toy.
8. Golf is a gentleman's game. Use your golf car with that thought in mind. Remember that pedestrians still have the right-of-way on the course, so don't push the foursome walking ahead of you.
9. Accelerate slowly.
10. Apply brakes gradually.
11. Love that golf course.

ADVANTAGES TO THE COURSE

1. Golf cars will increase revenue of your club.
2. They'll take the play away from courses which don't operate cars.
3. They'll allow many less robust members to play more and enjoy their game.
4. They'll allow many 9-hole players to play 18 by speeding up play.
5. They'll relieve the caddy shortage.
6. They'll lengthen the season (when caddies are less available.)

I've written this for The **WORTHINGTON MOWER COMPANY,** Stroudsburg, Pa. — a Subsidiary of Jacobsen Manufacturing Company, Racine, Wisconsin.

THE COMMERCIAL

This spread is made possible by my sponsor—the makers of the Worthington CHAMP Golf Car. Reprints are available for posting on your club bulletin board, write for them today.

Worthington was the logical builder of golfdom's ultimate golf car. When Worthington people set out to build a golf car that would be kind to terrain and comfortable for passengers, they called upon their vast experience gained in over 40 years of manufacturing golf course maintenance equipment.

The Worthington CHAMP Car has extra large, powerful 24 volts, 200 ampere hour batteries and a drive that is gradual and does not spin wheels. The Worthington CHAMP *does not take divots!*

It has automotive-type, internal-expansion brakes which come down gradually — no jolts. Feather-light steering tiller.

It has spring suspension built for perfect rider comfort.

SERVICE: Perhaps most important of all, this CHAMP car enjoys the use of the already existing Worthington golf course equipment service organization, throughout the country.

If your club permits privately-owned cars, you can buy your own Worthington CHAMP for $915. Charger and crating extra. (Charging costs only a few cents for 18 holes.)

little ad-ventures

by don herold

AND HE'S SO FINE OTHERWISE

Beat them to this criticism

Once in a lifetime is once too often for any man to commit the mistake that Mum can prevent.

I don't need to hem and haw about the bush. We all perspire. So far, so good. But, though the world grants this, it expects each man to keep his perspiration 100% shushed . . . mum . . . purely personal.

One breeze of it to the world, and he's declassé . . . out . . . a perspiration pariah.

So, if it were necessary, any man could afford the expense of using BARRELS of Mum to insure himself against committing this social blunder. But barrels aren't necessary. A tiny dab . . . a mere touch . . . under each arm after your bath each morning, and again before evenings out, is all that is required.

If Mum were hard to take it might be a different story. But Mum is a pleasant, fragrant, stainless cream, and a small jar lasts many weeks. It does not stop perspiration . . . simply acts as an all-day deodorant. Many men enjoy the habit of underarm touches of Mum, and many use Mum also for foot comfort, and to keep hose and shoe linings fresh. (Lots of druggists now report 1 out of 4 Mum sales to men.)

Be your own severest critic in this matter. Forestall comment by others.

I suggest an experiment. Try Mum at no expense. Send your name and address on this here adjacent margin and get a free sample. Mail to Bristol-Myers Co., Dept. G-85, 74 West St., New York City.

pencil here

Don Herold Says:

"Don't be the Goat of a Whispering Campaign"

Don't think for a minute that women don't talk—and talk right out—about such things.

Just let a man forget himself for one evening and come to a dance or a bridge game or a party with a slight case of perspiration fumes, and his name is Mr. Goat.

The girls sit on his case and hang him in the Hall of Shame.

Years after, Edna may say to Mable: "Remember that night in 1933 Ed Snootz came to the Club Dance with that cave-man aroma?"

There's only one sure-fire insurance against this kind of kitty-kat criticism. Bathe hard and cinch the good effects of your bath with dabs of Mum underarm.

Thousands of men now make Mum a daily after-bath habit, and use it invariably again before evenings out. Many also use touches to the feet to keep hose and shoe linings fresh.

Mum is a cream with a pleasant fragrance. It is harmless to shirts, it definitely kills perspiration odor for hours without stopping perspiration.

The start is the tough part. It's human to stall off such things. Why not take the jump now by sending your name on the margin of this page for a free sample to Bristol-Myers Company, Dept. S-49, 630-A Fifth Ave., New York City?

MUM TAKES **THE ODOR OUT OF PERSPIRATION**

COLUMNS GET READERS

One trick for getting longer copy across is to put it in *column* form, as if you expected it to be read, and to put in some humor (to repay the readers for reading on). Americans love to read newspaper columns, and many tests have proved that this goes too for advertisements in column form.

✓ ✓

I wrote these Mum ads for the Bristol-Myers Company and the hidden hint in the last paragraph to send for a sample brought so many requests that the column lasted for *six* years. (ORIGINAL AGENCY: *The Thompson-Koch Co.*) —*d.h.*

✓ ✓

These ads were, I believe, the first ads ever written to suggest that men should use a deodorant. This is perhaps my greatest claim to fame—that I am to some extent the father of the use of deodorants by men. Put this on my headstone, along with "I told you I was no hypochondriac." —*d.h.*

94

A chronic insomniac myself, I have always jumped at the chance to write soporific mattress copy, and have somehow become involved in a lot of it in my time. I've become something of a mattress authority in the process, and have, I believe, helped thousands to find more restful slumber. —d.h.

✓ ✓

One column that has endured successfully for many years is that of Old Fitzgerald bourbon, signed by Julian P. Van Winkle, president of Stitzel-Weller, the company which makes it. The columns are 100 proof, just like the bourbon. (AGENCY: *Winius-Brandon Company*)

✓ ✓

Single columns may be even better than double columns, because they look less like advertising and more like reading matter.

✓ ✓

Another reason for single columns versus double columns is that they cost half as much!

Sleepless Town

New York is a nice place to visit but is probably the hardest city in the world in which to get a good night's sleep.

So we thought there'd be room for *one* fine store in these parts which specialized in the very best sleeping equipment the world affords.

We looked the manufacturers over—slept on their mattresses—and chose Simmon's—starring the famous *Beautyrest* at $39.50, but offering other mattress marvels up to $100.

If you *must* live in New York, give yourself every possible break on sleep equipment.

You'd be justified in wrapping yourself in goopher feathers in this town, but *that* isn't necessary when you have, for example, a Simmon's *Beautyrest* for $39.50, with its 837 individual, silent, resilient springs —tuned to your individual weight —which *give* and *give* and *give* to every turn of your body.

The most you can spend on a complete outfit of mattress and springs at Hale's is $185—which is plenty little to invest in the sleeping third of your life in this heathenish, insomniac city.

Hale's
SPECIALISTS
IN SLEEPING
EQUIPMENT
© 36

420 Madison Avenue

Farmers Market Today

... with FRED BECK

PRE-TESTED — It is the policy of this dept. not to be advertising anything at you that this dept. wouldn't go for itself. I mean if I say goody goody for Magee's peanut butter, made right here in the Farmers Market from duly constituted uptown peanuts, then you can bet your last pair of button boots that I am a peanut butter eater.

So — I'll say it. "Goody goody f o r Magee's peanut butter."

You see what I mean about the policy of this dept.? If you're not satisfied with what is advertised here, bring it back and I'll eat it, unless it's a shoe brush or an ear-ring, in which case I will shine with it or wear it.

Well — that should explain how Rover came into my life. The Feed-Rite Pet Shop in here was in line for a puppy advertisement. Rover cost me $12.50 a pound, which isn't much for such a high class cocker dog as Rover, who weighed two pounds F.O.B. last Saturday, not counting the package.

BARGAIN DOGS — There is no ceiling price on dogs. The ceiling does not apply to dogs, and I will have no jokes about dogs applying to the floor.

The demand for dogs is not what it was, because people get thinking about meat rationing and all like that there, and there are fewer takers for dogs. Rover would have been a fifty-dollar job two years back, and if you want to buy a dog, you can now practically get two for the price of one if you come in early next Saturday before the selection of cocker dogs is all sold. (Nearly every Saturday the Feed-Rite Pet Shop has one basket of dogs. Limit, five to a customer.)

SATISFACTION — If Rover had turned out to be a son of a gun and no good, I would not herewith be advertising dogs. He is a good dog, and the ergo on this is that you can depend on a Farmers Market dog. Just what you d e p e n d on him to do I wouldn't know — but you can depend on him.

Training a small dog is a cinch. Rover can already walk on his hands, if you hold his hind legs up. But you don't want a trick dog because they b e c o m e facetious, like small girls who are in the movies.

Rover already understands about being a gentleman, and the way this was done was by c o n c e n t r a t i n g on the training job. Providing you know more than the dog, you can train him. Rover being exceptionally intelligent, and you know me kids, you can see where in the case of Rover's training things hung in the balance there for a minute.

VICTORY — The thing to do is to be prepared to devote about 24 hours straight to training a pup. This is harder on the pup than on you, because the poor thing is bewildered at being pried from his mother and he's just generally confused. Yet you must bear down and convey one simple thought to him. He will get the idea soon, and you can get it from Weiss when you buy your dog.

The job is easily done, especially when the weather is right and going outside is pleasant. Last Sunday Jupiter was Pluviusing all over the place, yet even at that the training job was completed successfully.

Besides dogs the Farmers Market has mustard, wieners, honey, olives, s t e a k s and chops, dog collars and corn flakes. Also a location: W. 3rd at Fairfax.

Among the most amusing and most effective columns ever written were those by Fred Beck in Los Angeles newspapers for the internationally famous Farmers Market in Los Angeles—founded by Roger Dahlhjelm in 1934 and now boasting over 165 separate shops, perhaps the original pilot model of the modern shopping center.

Fred Beck's trick was to belittle the merchandise. Typically: "Our tomatoes are tasteless. We'll let you know when they are good again." Readers liked this frankness and jammed the stalls of the market.

this is our great big
huge enormous gigantic
annual sale

Ours is the only genuine Annual Sale in town.

We call it an Annual Sale because it lasts 52 weeks a year. It started November 23, and it's liable to keep going for the next 44 years. It will, that is, if old man Gillette can keep going for 44 years and he says he's going to try.

Now let us give you a little data.

Also, a smattering of disa.

Some stores only have sales during slow months. Us, we run up the sale flags every single month. We don't have sale prices one month and regular prices another month. Fine thing if we couldn't make up our minds how much to charge our customers.

We figure if a $145 suit can be sold for $103.30 next July, then that's what it should be sold for in January.

Also February.

Not to mention March, April and May. And all the other months. If a store always has to have a clearance to

Actually, our boss is probably more guilty than any other boss in town. He buys about 10 times too many suits, and then he has to have a sale every month to get rid of them all.

In fact, Mr. Gillette's cardiac area has gotten awfully soft. Instead of cutting prices on maybe 8½% of his stock, he cuts the prices on 100% of his stock.

In fact, he can't wait a year or two. He cuts the prices as fast as the stuff comes in.

If others want to be part-time price cutters on only a few of their suits, that's their business. Jules will keep right on being the worst price cutter in town.

There are only two kinds of Annual Sale. Ours, and the other kind.

Our Annual Sale is not for schnooks and mummsers, and men who wear their ties au gratin. It's for men who know the very finest clothing when they see it. And

I lost the Jules Gillette name plate

606 N.E. 125TH ST. IN NORTH MIAMI
Where N.E. 6th Ave. & Dixie Hwy. intersect 125th St.
Our doors stay locked on Mon., Tues., Wed.
Open Thurs. & Fri., 9:30 to 9:30; Sat. 9 to 6
Sundays 11 to 5:30 (come over after church)

Top of a full two-column ad—one of a series of terrifically daring and unconventional (and humorous) ads by Jules Gillette, Miami clothier, who left high-rent Lincoln Road for the northern outskirts of Miami at 606 N.E. 125th Street, and announced closing on Mondays, Tuesdays, and Wednesdays and 28 per cent off on all fine nationally known brands of men's clothing. Bottom of the ads was full of listings of examples of brand-name suits at special Gillette prices. Written refreshingly by Phil Lansdale, who calls himself Mr. Gillette's psychiatrist.

I THOUGHT TIRES GREW ON TREES

by don herold

● I've always thought that tires were pretty simple things.

I mean, I thought you tapped a rubber tree, got some rubber, melted it, molded it...and had your tire.

But, gee-whillikens, I have just been through the big Kelly-Springfield tire factory at Cumberland, Md., and I've learned that "mixing" a tire is 100 times more complicated than baking a cake.

KELLY CARBON BLACK MIXING IS THE NUB OF IT

There are some 30 ingredients in the "rubber" of a Kelly tire—not just rubber, as I'd always thought.

The most important of these (next to rubber) is *carbon black,* and the exceptional toughness of Kelly tires is due largely to the special process the Kelly people have developed for mixing and remixing a greater quantity of carbon black more thoroughly and evenly into and throughout their rubber compound.

Carbon is the hardest known abrasive resistant in the world.(A diamond, you know, is merely a form of carbon.) Well, this carbon black in Kelly tires is produced by burning gas flames against cold metal plates, but that is neither here nor there.

I HOPE I'M TIRING YOU

The point is that—as used in a Kelly tire—carbon black produces a tire so tough it will wear out a piece of steel.

So...in Kelly tires...you get treads which are literally *pliable armor plate.* That's why they call them Kelly ARMORUBBER tires.

Kelly's great 44-year reputation for "class quality" has attracted a fine group of dealers. The Kelly man in your neighborhood will give you reliable, friendly tire advice when you next feel new tires coming on.

IF BATTLESHIPS HAD TIRES—

by don herold

● I suppose we've all dreamt of inventing *iron* tires as soft as *rubber.*

Maybe it would be possible to put steel fish scales on the outside of tires—and ideas like that.

Well, the average layman (like myself) would be surprised if he knew how close a certain tire manufacturer has come to mixing steel and rubber in the same tire compound.

Fact is, this manufacturer has gone steel one better.

The toughest known abrasive resistant in the world is carbon. Some types of carbon are used to make steel tougher. (A diamond is merely a kind of carbon.)

Somebody discovered that if you mix molecules of *carbon black* with molecules of rubber, it will lengthen the life of a tire by thousands of miles.

Ever since a famous movie star (years ago) smiled sweetly through the middle of a Kelly tire, I've had the impression that Kellys were about the best mileage tires money could buy.

Today I find Kellys cost no more than other good tires, but I believe they can outlast many other makes many miles and I'll tell you why.

Kelly scientists have developed a special way of mixing a greater amount of *carbon black* far more evenly and thoroughly into and throughout their rubber compound. Because of this, a Kelly tire will outwear the toughest steel ever made.

A Kelly tire is really a pliable armor plate. That is why Kelly treads are logically and fairly called *Armorubber.*

The 44-year Kelly reputation for long wear has attracted so many of the top-notch tire dealers of this country, that you can always count on getting a fine tire and a fair deal from a Kelly dealer.

Most tire ads consist mainly of immense pictures of tires—the immenser the better—and blackface type to punch you in the eye. But I found, on visiting the Kelly-Springfield factory, that there are real reasons why Kellys are better than lots of tires, and the Kelly-Springfield people agreed that it was worth a number of quarter-page tries to tell these reasons to a lot of tiretired motorists, and they found in time that this quiet process had really sold a lot of tires. —d.h. (AGENCY: *J. Stirling Getchell, Inc.*)

Humor in Retail Advertising

Retail advertising may offer more examples of humor, because it has less time to work itself up into a stew of disastrous solemnity.

It has better chances for spontaneity because it is subject to fewer committee meetings. There is time for fewer second thoughts. And the costs are less.

A lot of advertising would be better if it went off half-cocked.

Perhaps the most delightful uses of humorous advertising ever made are in the advertisements and bulletins of Fortnum & Mason, London grocers. We've never had any advertising like it in America, so we've never had any grocery store to equal it in America. I'm giving several examples of pages from Fortnum & Mason's "Commentaries" in this volume; I could fill this whole book with their copy. The writing is classic. English humor is more delicate than ours, so English advertising humor can safely be more gossamer than ours.

Here, from their calendar of the years, are some examples of Fortnum & Mason fun:

1749. Will Noblemen refrain from testing our cheese with their swords? Goodly skewers are provided for the purpose and it is beyond question that too many swords dishearten any cheese.

Under "Questing for Turkeys" in another Fortnum & Mason brochure, we find this:

Calling for our galoshes and a bag of oranges, we took coach for Norfolk in search of the very largest turkeys you ever heard of—and we have found them. It really is going to be a proper Christmas this year.

Arriving in Norfolk (we knew by the position of Sirius in the sky) we confronted these magnificent creatures, facing every peril for our customers' sake. We pitted ourselves against the largest to feel their fatness—sometimes we won, sometimes we didn't; but few turkeys flout us twice when once our blood is up. We held our own against the fleetest, even in our galoshes, and tied labels to their legs marked "F & M, their Bird."

Thirsty and a little shop-soiled, we returned to our coach—where the oranges awaited us—and so home; but mark our words these turkeys will stagger you.

One of Fortnum & Mason's most delightful whimsies is their insistence on maintaining their illusion of great age. The actual date of their founding is unknown, but they refer to themselves as having resided in "their great house in Piccadilly with great decency and undying hope since the second glacial age—approximately."

Then they speak of themselves as having existed during the Crusades, and as having, with their turtle soup for invalids, spurred the flabby barons into such health and activity that they wanted to be up and doing, hence bringing about the First Crusade.

It took us years to produce a turtle soup for invalids that expressed the beauty of the turtle's nature without its grossness. The spiced soup of the banqueting chamber is fit and proper fodder for aldermen in rude health, but our invalid turtle soup is a thing apart. A soup freed from fats and unspiced. Dainty beyond compare and possessing a fragrance that heartens the most languid appetite. You cannot expect us to reveal the whole secret of its making, but this much we can say: Such soup as this cannot be made from elderly turtles of the worldly type—with doubtful pasts and wrinkles around the eyes. No! Impossible! Our invalid turtle soup is made exclusively from innocent little turtles, reared in the most

sheltered lagoons. Many daughters of the best turtle families voluntarily go into our soup to escape the world's rough badinage.

In an article written way back in 1926, Florence Brobeck, in commenting on Fortnum & Mason advertising, said:

Perhaps a group of copy writers, advisers, layout experts, art directors, general managers, vice-presidents and what not, meet in conference to haggle over this copy even as is done in American advertising agencies and offices. If this is the case it is by a miracle that the finished commentaries go forth with their undisputable air of spontaneity, their exaggerated but undeniable appeal to the appetite and purse. They leave the impression from their merry pictures that the foods are prepared in great sunny kitchens, by singing chefs and skilled, happy assistants. There is no dry paragraph to set forth that the soups were all stirred by so many thousands of revolving paddles, or that the chickens for chicken mousse were raised on such and such thousand-acre farms, or that the cookies were baked in the biggest, best, cleanest, quietest, etc., etc., bakery in the land.

In a recent charming letter to me, Charles Butler, director of Fortnum & Mason, pinpoints the founding date of the firm as 1707. He sent me a brochure which states: "William Fortnum fell in with a man called Mason. They didn't know it then, but in fact they had created a union surpassed in its importance to the human race only by the meeting of Adam with Eve."

Rogers Peet Company, successful East Coast men's clothiers, have been using cartoon ads for over eighty-five years. They were started and written for many years by Frank R. Chambers, one of the members of the firm. I often cite Rogers Peet's amazing consistency and continuity when an advertiser for whom I'm working gets nervous and wants to do "something different" for a "change of pace."

The best long-time consistent use of the light touch in retail advertising in America is the lovely copy (verse and prose) written for Macy's over a period of years by Margaret Fishback, when Kenneth Collins was her far-sighted mentor.

On other pages I've reproduced several of Margaret Fishback's prose ads for Macy's. Here is one of her poems from a full-page ad for them.

Best wishes
one and all!

A happy New Year to you and yours
From R. H. Macy, the largest of stores.
We wish you electric irons and toasters,
Velocipedes, radios, skates, and roasters,
And washing machines, and bikes, and sleds,
And innerspring mattresses for your beds,
Refrigerators, and cuckoo clocks,
Elastic girdles and evening socks,
And though it will make your bosom flutter,
May you have plenty of sugar and butter,
And nylons galore, your legs to flatter,
And massive roasts for your Sunday platter.
An apartment, too, with closets spacy,
The raiment inside, supplied by Macy.

We wish you health and we wish you cheer
From now straight on through the coming year.
May loved ones be united again,
May peace on earth and good will to men
Embrace this battered old world once more
And heal the terrible scars of war.
May the homes with empty places be
Solaced by warmth and sympathy.
May heavy hearts find surcease in
The victory that they helped to win.
And may we all of us breathe a prayer
Of thanks to show that we're well aware
How lucky we are to be here today
In our own beneficent U. S. A.

Gimbels made good use of humor in whimsical ads written for them by Stanley Jones. Jones later distinguished himself at Young & Rubicam for his gay copy for Gourmet Foods and for Sanforized.

Here are a few clips from Stanley Jones' trade ads on Sanforized:

In those days B. S. (before "Sanforized") the shirt-maker lived dangerously. He had to. Manufacturers tried all kinds of over-sizing, hoping to give a man a good fit *After Shrinkage*. Naturally, this mad gamble worked about as often as a sturgeon makes out his will.

The glamour flits away when the fit is gone.

Every man knows that "Sanforized" labeled shirts are forever and a day as comfortable as a cashmere bath mat.

Returns are ptomaine.

If you don't give people value today, you might as well save your breath to cool your soup.

A fitted sheet that doesn't stay a fitted sheet can be as hard on you as bird seed in your shoes.

One of the historically famous humorous retail ads of all time was the sensational "Manure" ad written for Gimbels by Bernice Fitz-Gibbon, long-time ad helmswoman at Gimbels, afterwards head of her own public relations organization. The copy went as follows:

No bossy but no bossy
has finer manure than Gimbels

You can take Gimbels out of the farm . . . but you can't take the farm out of Gimbels. In all the land there is not a street floor more chic, more radiant than Gimbels new street floor. And on this new street floor you won't find a more beautiful, more "bloomy" shop than Gimbels new Flower Shop. But even though our walls are elegantly pink and elegantly green, we're still realists at heart. There's always been something earthy . . . something from the soil . . . about Gimbels. And we can't forget that it's things like manure and compost and mulch that make our flowers so breath-takingly beautiful. Why, then, should anyone be startled to find us discussing the merits of organic nutrition in the same breath with modern decor and indirect lighting? Udderly ridiculous, say we. We think it's a bright-eyed idea to give someone manure for Christmas. Tickle the earth, say we, and she'll laugh a harvest. And that's the very reason we've made contact with our bovine friends in Westchester, Long Island, and New Jersey. We'll ship a magnificent 1-ton batch of Daisy's finest to your door (or to the rear door or the barn) for $19 (within 20 miles of Gimbels). Or, if you prefer organic and chemical mixture, we'll ship same in 50-pound bags for a paltry 2.79.

Jules Gillette, a high-class men's clothier of Miami Beach, caused a national sensation when he moved from high-rent Lincoln Road to the outskirts of Miami at 606 N.E. 125th Street and announced that he would be closed every Monday, Tuesday, and Wednesday, and would sell only the highest grade nationally known brands of men's clothes, and would have an all-year markdown of 28 per cent on everything in the store—for example, a $175 suit for $125.44.

His full-page announcement in the *Miami Herald* was followed a few days later by the following copy:

Jules Gillette fights back

Which are you, one of the ones who hates us, or one of the ones with such a brilliant mind that you don't hardly object to our advertising at all?

Oh brother, did we ever get blasted for that full page ad we had in the Herald Thursday.

Some readers actually complimented us on it. These were the ones with the brilliant minds, like we said. But others, well they were just horrified that anybody would do such a thing. Especially anybody old enough to know better.

Well, we did it, and we apologize to everybody, and now we're going to keep right on doing it, because it's a free country isn't it?

Besides, we can't think of any national or state law which says that men's clothing ads have to be dull and deadly. If you insist on being bored, read the other ads instead of ours and then you can't get offended at what we say.

Story *of* a 4th Baronet's love *for*
STILTON CHEESE

*W*HY DO CLUB STEWARDS COME TO US for Stiltons and yet more Stiltons, while members pace their smoking-rooms with burning eyes, saying, " Major, can you see him coming yet ? "

It is because ours are *real* Stiltons, made by the Yeomen families of Leicestershire from recipes that have been their secret for generations. These are the only Stiltons that count. They are rare enough in these days, but we have them. Let no man think he knows the Stilton ecstasy if he has only eaten Stiltons from factories where steam hisses from every cranny and pale youths make sport with milk-cans.

It was only last week, at the ―― Club (name deleted by Censor), that one of our real Stiltons had become deeply dug, and a 4th Baronet, in the course of his investigations, got his head fixed in the tall circle of the rind. When the Marquis of ―― and the wine-waiter rushed to free him, the 4th Baronet's muffled voice was heard saying, "Leave me here, I like it." This gives you some idea.

4th Baronet refusing to be extricated from the Stilton Cheese

Perhaps the greatest and sweetest and most successful use of humor over many years has been that of Fortnum & Mason, London grocers extraordinary. I could devote this whole book to reproductions of their supreme work. They are the Shakespeare of delightful whimsy in advertising. —d.h.

A SWEET RETREAT ABOVE THE WORLD ✌

Some day we will show you our olive groves on the slopes of the Maritime Alps, dreaming in that queer French silence, where no birds sing, and only distant goat-bells break the silence.

Far below lies the world with motor roads and casinos and things, but, up here, there is nothing but sunshine and clear air, and a quiet wayside shrine where devout goat-herds plant their little candles.

Our olive oil is pure sunshine—made from olives so nourishing that a handful will sustain a peasant the livelong day. These same peasants gather the olive harvest for us and take it to the crushing, where the juice is run into porcelain tanks, making olive oil golden as a buttercup's petal and most exquisitely delicate of flavour. Olive oil most fit to grace your salad or give blessed strength to an invalid.

It gives strength to Invalids

"HOT STUFF."

Overcoats for $10 for large boys and small men (30 to 34 inches round the chest), reduced from $18 and $20.

Good warm chinchilla and ratine, not quite fashionable length—that's why they're $10.

ROGERS, PEET & CO.

THREE | Prince,
BROADWAY } Warren,
STORES. | 32d St.

The New-York Times.

NEW-YORK, SATURDAY, MAY 6, 1882.

THOSE DARNED OLD SOX

OR OLD DARNED SOCKS WERE PRETTY WELL DILAPIDATED BY LAST SUMMER'S WEAR, AND TO A MAN OF NERVOUS TEMPERAMENT IT IS SOMEWHAT VEXATIOUS NOT TO FIND HIS CLOTHES IN PERFECT ORDER WHEN WANTED FOR IMMEDIATE USE—BETTER HAVE SOME NEW ONES RIGHT AWAY.

MEN IN EVERY STATE OF DILAPIDATED AP-PAREL WOULD BETTER COME DIRECT TO US AND BE PROPERLY CLOTHED INSTEAD OF LOSING TIME AND TEMPER SEARCHING IN VA-RIOUS SMALL STORES FOR ANY NEEDED ARTICLE OF DRESS. OUR "FIXINGS" DEPARTMENT IS ALMOST AS POPULAR AS OUR BIG DEPARTMENT FOR BOYS' CLOTHING WHERE "FIXINGS" AND HATS, TOO, ARE KEPT.

IF TO-DAY IS PLEASANT WE SHALL EXPECT A CROWD, AND WILL REMAIN HERE UNTIL 10 O'CLOCK TO-NIGHT TO WAIT UPON LATE SHOP-PERS.

Rogers, Peet & Co.,

CLOTHIERS AND FURNISHERS,

569-575 BROADWAY,

OPPOSITE

METROPOLITAN HOTEL.

Rogers Peet Company, New York clothiers, have done mighty well by using cartoons and light-vein copy, usually in small space, since 1882. They shame other advertisers who got nervous and serious and scared after a short trial of humor. The ads were written for many years by one of the partners of the firm, Frank R. Chambers. The cartoons have been done by many famous cartoonists, including Bob Wildhack, Forbell, and even for a while, John Barrymore!

One spot favored by Rogers Peet over the years is theatre programs, in bright ads tied up somehow with the show. Here's one that goes way back to the Floradora Sextette.

Rogers Peet —OPEN THURSDAYS—
Our Fifth Avenue Stores
are open Thursdays 'til 8:30

Still Searching?

Still, with only four shopping days left, looking for that Just Right gift for Father's Day? Solution: A Rogers Peet Gift Certificate!

You'll be in good company . . . for many doting dependents use this fine means of letting Dad choose what he really needs and wants in our fine stores.

Clincher: It's proof positive that every cent you borrowed from him was used for his gift!

Makers and Merchants of Fine Clothes for Gentlemen since 1874

Rogers Peet company
NEW YORK — BOSTON
WASHINGTON

Fifth Avenue | Fifth Avenue | 258 Broadway
at 48th Street | at 41st Street | at Warren Street

Boston: Tremont at Bromfield St.
Washington: 14th & G Sts., N. W.

FLORODORA.

What's the use of telling pretty maidens — we sell only clothing, furnishings, hats and shoes for men and boys?

Rogers Peet & Co.
258-842-1260 Broadway— , Stores
New York

"Why not <u>sleep</u> at Macy's too, and save coal?"

Logical Louie wants to know why the Little Woman *ever* comes home from the World's Largest Store. She spends practically every day there, and Thursday nights till 9. If she could only arrange to have the family move into a suite of Macy's model rooms on the Furniture Floor, Louie figures they wouldn't need to burn any coal at all. Not that he resents her devotion to Macy's. Far from it! He says Heaven knows he'd rather let her run loose at Macy's than anywhere else, in these taxing times, when everyone *needs* to save. For good old Macy's not only saves him coal. Macy's 85-year-old, low-for-cash price policy and mammoth assortments keep his standard of living *up* and his cost of living *down*.

Now more than ever, it's smart to be thrifty. **macy's**

Perhaps the most outstanding job of humorous retail advertising done in America were those ads created, in verse and prose, by Margaret Fishback for Macy's. Here are three she did in conjunction with artist Jack Skolnik in *The New Yorker*.

6 Easy Ways to Save Money

In this difficult era of mounting taxes and rising costs, *everyone* feels the urge to save. Substantial savings may be effected in many ways, such as . . .

1. Give up wearing clothes. If you don't wear them, they won't wear out. Thus you won't need to replace them.

2. Do without shaves and haircuts, finger waves and manicures.

3. Give up eating and drinking.

4. Sell your furniture and stand up.

5. Live in the Park, and save rent altogether.

6. Walk, don't ride.

Take your pick, pals. But if you feel these methods are too rigorous or im-practical, there's still another way of conserving cash. That is, shop in the World's Largest Store, and get that very special money's worth for which Macy's is famous. Macy's, thrift specialist of 84 years' standing, provides the things you need at prices you can afford to pay. *Now more than ever, it's smart to be thrifty.* **macy's**

Another Margaret Fishback

The Feminine Touch

We never used to approve of wives who felt Spring housecleaning included a methodical check-up of Papa's pants' pockets. But in times like these, when *everyone* feels the need to save, a little teeny weeny bit of larceny seems justifiable at certain moments. In this lady's case, the moment has come when she hears the still, soft voice of Macy's calling her. She can no longer resist the urge to buy herself a new pair of shoes. Her old ones have been resoled so often, the cobbler claims he will have to make tops to go with the soles next time.

So we don't blame her for taking steps. Nor will her mate, when he knows she spent his dough in New York's most popular store, where ninety-four cents acts like an overgrown dollar.

Now more than ever, it's smart to be thrifty. **macy's**

Another Margaret Fishback

"Why, the Hussy!"

LIKE a page from that gay and lively pictorial "La Vie Parisienne" is a certain new model brassiere which Gimbels Fourth Floor is now showing.

We are not skilled in descriptive reporting along these lines, but even a Hottentot could discern that this particular flimsy was designed for dash, rather than for seal-hunting in the cold, cold North. We were told that it was the latest French model, which doubles our hope that we may live another year or two, at least. However—

"It hasn't any real name," a salesgirl informed us. "But just between us, here on the floor, we got 'to calling it 'The Hussy.' You know—just in fun."

"Sure," we said. "No sense in taking things too seriously. Many sales?"

She thought a moment, then laughed.

"The other day a prim-looking lady happened to see one of them. She asked what it was called, and, before I thought, I said, 'We call it 'The Hussy.'' She got real red, stared at it a moment, then tossed up her head and marched out."

"You killed the sale, eh?" we said.

The girl laughed again. "I thought so, all right. But about twenty minutes later my phone rang and a voice said, 'Send up one of those new, er, Hussy brassieres to this address, please, and charge it.' She tried to disguise her voice, but I caught it at once."

Please, don't get Gimbels wrong! We also sell any number of old-fashioned nightcaps—pink ribbons and all! But, if you really feel that way about it, the Hussy's 82.

GIMBELS

33RD & BROADWAY

Carilloneur

TOUCHING are the lengths to which nostalgia occasionally drives a man:

He was French. Small, and neat, and wistful of eye. And while the sales girls were busy at the far end of Gimbels first floor clock counter, he noodled hopefully among the flotilla of alarm clocks. One would clang—instantly he would cut it off.

Finally he worked into a batch that chimed.

"Ah!" he exclaimed happily. "Ah, c'est ca!"

He set off one. Then another. Then two at once. Head cocked, eyes half-closed, absorbing the assorted notes.

When the girl reached him, there were four sets of chimes bonging away, and he was happy as a clam at high tide.

In his home village, he explained, there was a carillon—a small set of bells—in a tower. They were supposed to chime away the lazy hours and—of a Sunday—to send forth a few simple airs. In the old days they awakened him, instead of battering clocks—and trolleys. But now, a friend had bought one of these, with chimes, and was *enchante* with it. Reminded him . . .

"But," said the girl, considerably touched, "these are cheap clocks, you know. They may not all go off at the same time."

"Pooh!" he said. That made no difference; it was the reminder he wanted, the chime. Sometimes, in his village, the carilloneur was half an hour late. He thought—a thousand pardons, mam'selle—that *les Americains* sometimes took the matter of time pretty seriously, anyhow. And he'd take the four clocks . . .

Pleasant notes—new notes—are being struck all through this fine old store these days. Drop in. You, too, will be "enchante"!

GIMBELS

33rd & BROADWAY

These two ads were in a long series written for Gimbels, New York department store, by Stanley Jones, one of America's most blithesome copywriters, later noted for his outstanding copy for Young & Rubicam on Sanforized and on Gourmet Foods.

The horse with the hansom behind...

That's the horse that <u>didn't</u> come to Gimbels even back in the days when hansoms and cabbies flourished. Plain old Gimbels never got the carriage trade. The well-heeled set that put on airs and lived like nabobs, liked to do their shopping in an elegant lush plush establishment. Gimbels never was elegant, ain't elegant now and (we suspect) never will be elegant. For 101 years Gimbels has had the horse and buggy trade— the millions of solid, solvent, substantial Americans who have always let down hems, saved candle ends, counted pennies, checked prices, and demanded every copper's worth of value whether they were spending a buck or a sawbuck. 101 years of dealing with these thrift experts have taught us that thrift consists of buying only what you need when you need it. This New York Times carries 3 pages of Gimbels bargains ranging from seersucker at 69c (one yard) to a Van Dyck at $79,000 (about 3 yards). But don't buy either or anything else unless you need it. We're glad we didn't get the horse with the hansom behind—we prefer the horse with the buggy behind.

Bernice Fitz-Gibbon, long-time genius advertising manager of Gimbels, wrote this classic on the kind of people who used to stay away from plain old Gimbels. She describes the horse-and-buggy people who did and *do* come to Gimbels, and says Gimbels always did prefer the horse with the buggy behind to the horse with the hansom behind. This copy is hard to read because of its lack of paragraphs, but it's well worth reading from start to finish.

"Look! Mr. Jones has a new Knox Hat!"

Woolf Brothers

A fine long-time series of humorous and sophisticated retail ads are those created by George L. Cartlich for Woolf Brothers of Kansas City, Mo. They are usually of the one-line caption variety. (ARTIST: *Jack O'Hara*)

111

Even Scrooge Would Be Happy

With A Gift Bond From

Woolf Brothers

Give Him a Break

(AMONG OTHER THINGS)

● Father will not come out this Sunday (Father's Day), look at his shadow (in the mirror) and scamper back to his hole in shame—not if you will choose his Father's Day gifts at Stern's Store for Men. For example, he'll actually strut with pride if you'll garb him in one of the splendid Neckties of finer imported silks that we are offering this week in a record-breaking sale at 59c. Or if he has sufficient ties, maybe he'd prefer :

French Back Silk Shorts.........3 *for* 4.00	Japanese Silk Pajamas.................5.00
Lisle Hose, desirable patterns.......pr. 45c	Striped Oxford Summer Robe..........4.00
Sterncrest Shirts.....................1.95	Tie-Clasp and Collar Pin.............2.00

STERN'S STORE FOR MEN appeals to men because men recognize it as a thoroughly masculine store in itself, not as an afterthought to a woman's store. That, incidentally, makes it a good place for women to shop for men's things. And that probably explains why it has grown with such masculine strides the past year...along with the remainder of Stern's. Men may reach our Store for Men direct from entrances on Sixth Avenue and on Forty-third Street. It is on the main floor, right off the street, easily reached without traipsing through corridors of women's things or jostling package-laden shoppers in the elevators.

Stern Brothers
STORE FOR MEN
FORTY-SECOND STREET, WEST OF FIFTH AVENUE

by *d.h.* for a New York department store

do you think our advertising should be more serious?

Before you answer that, we'd better explain what we're trying to accomplish.

We do sell men's top quality clothing, from America's most respected manufacturers. It's expensive clothing. And no other store in Florida sells anything better, regardless of what they charge.

We sell this clothing at prices which are considerably less than you can find in any other store.

It is customary for any men's store that sells expensive clothing to take from 45% to 60% profit margin on the selling price.

We take less than 30% on everything in the house.

What does that mean to you? It means that a conventional, well-managed store that buys a suit which costs them $58.90, for example, will sell it anywhere from $110 up to $135. Thus their profit margin on the selling price will be anywhere from 46.5% to 56.4%.

When we buy that suit for $58.90, we sell it for $84.04. That is exactly 29.9% profit margin on the selling price.

You might ask, who is kidding who? How can we stay in business if we cut prices like that? We do it by selling nothing except better clothing. No shirts. No socks. No garters. No pajamas. And then, we have to sell ten times as much of this better clothing as any other store that has our same overhead.

Now then, how do we make you understand the way we run our business? And how do we make you believe it is really true?

The woods around here are full of stores, including some highly regarded ones, that make surprisingly careless, exaggerated claims about the "regular" prices and how much money they're saving you.

There is not one store in all of Florida, or between here and Maine for all we know, that is selling men's high quality clothing for anywhere near 30% margin. Not a one.

But how can we get this information across to you?

Not by big black screaming headline claims. They won't work, for two reasons.

(1) Exaggerated price claims are a penny a dozen in Miami. If we came out with big blasts about our prices, who would believe us? We would just put ourselves in exactly the same boat as other stores, whereas we are not the same as other stores at all.

(2) Thus we would have to run bigger ads, and more ads, than anybody else, to hammer you into trying us instead of them. If we spent that kind of money to drive you over here by brute force, then we'd have to increase our prices to pay the cost of doing that. And then we wouldn't be a bit better than anybody else.

No sir. What we have to use is some method of exposing you to our message, and getting you to understand what we have here. We figure that by making our ads interesting and imaginative, we will get you to read them. Then, by appealing to your logic and reason, we'll eventually get you here through curiosity, if nothing else.

Our advertising has to be more efficient, and create more sales per dollar spent, than any other advertising in the paper.

When we list specific items and prices in our ads, we tell you the going price in other stores. You can then compare it with our selling price. The facts are not doctored to make our prices look better than they really are. Sooner or later you will learn that the facts are what we say they are.

And that our prices are at least 28% under the prices elsewhere.

We're not out for the fast buck. Instead of trying to make a sale, we're trying to acquire a customer.

We hope you'll enjoy reading our ad every Saturday in the Herald. And we hope that sooner or later you'll drive over here and find out the facts for yourself.

Today. Next week. Or next month.

The freshest note in retail advertising for some time is that of Jules Gillette, Miami, far-out men's clothier (in more ways than one). Read one of his ads and you're pretty sure to read them all. His policy is to sell the highest priced men's clothing at 28 per cent less than usual prices, or even less. He is on the north edge of Miami, and is open only on four days a week, and boasts that he sells no shirts, no socks, no garters, no pajamas.

our dog shop
which recently
made its

bow

is a

wow!

JUST INSIDE THE BIG DOOR ON 43rd ST.
EVERYTHING FROM BISCUITS TO BASKETS

Stern Brothers

42nd STREET, WEST OF FIFTH AVENUE

by *d.h.* for a New York department store

It's not our doorman's birthday

● It's not even OURS.

In fact, you'll find it more like YOUR birthday than OURS, here in June—with all these lovely Summer things we have for you and at THESE PRICES !

● We could have asked our doorman if he or his Aunt Emma was having a birthday that we could celebrate here in June, or found some other typical excuse . . . but we decided to go at this June Event Series entirely from *your* angle.

What things does our public need in June? For how little can we sell these things? What can we give our customers to celebrate . . . instead of *our* birthday or *our* tin wedding or *our* Whatsis?

● We concluded that what the world craves *now* is bargains in cool June things, Summer things, beach things, home things, lawn things, porch things and such—freshly purchased, style-lively merchandise right off the ice.

That is the idea behind this Series of June Events at Stern's.

● Let June, then, bring you bounding to the attractive "new Stern's." Come and feel the new life that vibrates in this fine new-old store from basement to roof. Roam our breezy Beach Club and swanky Sports Shop on our Third Floor—our Summer Furniture Shop on the Seventh—our Sweater'n Slack Shop for boys on the Second—our Game Shop and Men s Beach Shop (and, yes, our Dog Shop) on the Main.

Make a whole day of it soon one of these June days . . . at Stern's. Lunch refreshingly in our bright Fifth Floor restaurant. *And watch every inch of Stern's advertising in June.*

Stern Brothers
42nd Street, West of Fifth Avenue

Spoofing the custom of retail stores of finding absurd excuses for sales. Here's a sale that is simply a sale for sake of a sale—merely incidentally a June sale. —*d.h.*

Remember "modernistic" furniture?

Back in the '20s, when most of the modern designs in America

were still between the covers of imported books and magazines,

Macy's opened the first modern furniture department in the country.

On the day the department opened it showed only authentic modern,

and from that day on it has never shown anything else.

Macy's Forward House was one place where you never

could buy the corkscrew tables, fullback sofas

and struck-by-lightning lamps that got to be called

"modernistic" (with a humorous twist on the -istic)

"Modernistic" was news, a style with all the temporary glamour of a crazy hat.

Macy's never showed it because we felt

you mightn't like owning it once the furore died down.

(And die, it did—before you could say "I'll take vanilla.")

Today we feel about modern furniture pretty much the way

we felt about it in 1927 when we sent our buyers abroad

to bring the first fine modern back to America. We feel

that every design isn't necessarily good because it's new,

or valid because it's unusual. We know that,

to be a good investment, furniture must be timeless enough to survive

a hundred fads. That's why you won't find

every conceivable kind of modern in Forward House.

That's why you *will* find large assortments of tried-and-true modern,

and of the most recent pieces that are bound to become classics.

You'll find furniture made especially for us: furniture

that is structurally honest, beautiful, and therefore good

for years to come. That's more important than ever today,

when you're buying for the future.

Forward House, Macy's Ninth Floor.

You couldn't buy it at Macy's

★ **MACY'S PRICE POLICY:** *We endeavor to have the prices of our merchandise reflect a six per cent saving for cash, except on price-fixed merchandise.*

An ad which sells modern furniture by kidding "modernistic" furniture.

THE GREATEST SPORTING GOODS STORE IN THE WORLD

B TOBEY—

"And while you're moored at Hyannis Port..."

While A&F can outfit you with the best in basic needs for any sport, we also offer many things designed "just for fun." Consequently every trip to A&F becomes good sport in itself.

Men's Laminated Yacht Parka. A new idea in comfort. Rugged blue cotton denim bonded to polyester foam to keep you dry and warm. **24.50**

Seafarer Grill. Regardless of roll, this grill stays level! Gimbals and quick-detach bracket fasten to bulkhead. Aqua porcelain bowl with chrome trim and ash catcher. **34.95**

Thermal Tumblers. Double-wall design keeps drinks cold longer, will not sweat. Choice of nautical knots, real fish flies and sailboats. Set of four old-fashioned or highball. . **12.00**

Top-Sider Oxford. Protects you and the deck. White canvas with cushion insole, squeegee rubber sole. Men's and women's. **9.95**

Mail and phone orders accepted

Abercrombie & Fitch

360 MADISON AVENUE, NEW YORK

CHICAGO   COLORADO SPRINGS   SAN FRANCISCO
BAY HEAD   SOUTHAMPTON   HYANNIS

It's right that Abercrombie & Fitch, a store that specializes in fun apparel and fun equipment, should use fun in its advertising. Here's a good combination of humor (at the top) and catalog merchandising at the bottom.

A nationwide survey shows I'd be happier with money

Humor in
Financial Advertising

Strange, but banks, insurance companies, and other financial institutions have been pioneers in using humor in advertising, and many of them have been consistent at it for years.

"Because humor does have a humanizing effect, if nothing else, it would seem logical that banks and insurance companies, traditional suffers from a stuffy image, should have been among the first to try the light touch," writes *Printers' Ink*.

Though financial institutions realized early and wisely that the first thing they must do to win public confidence was to establish an impression of solidity and permanence, with granite façades and the use of bronze and brass, many of them must have learned that in designing their buildings they had gone too far in the direction of mausoleums, and were scaring great sections of the public away. They reasoned that a little unbending in ads could decrease the mortuary effect to some extent and help establish them as nice, helpful guys instead of inaccessible, glass-eyed ogres.

To a convention of officials of savings and loan associations a few years ago, I said:

You are in one of the most human businesses in the world today. Yet you sometimes become so involved in the mathematics and technical problems of your business, that you may forget entirely the good things you are really doing for people.

Consequently you may let your advertising become far more icy than your business itself.

You may forget, even, why people want to save money in the first place. They want to save money, not because it's money, but because they can some-day do something very human with it—have some fun—take a trip—buy a new car—pay for a new baby

I'm going to improve my social security

SAVINGS

—start a little business—start to buy a new home—have some safety—pay a doctor or hospital bill—send

a child to school—help out a married son or daughter—weather a period when ordinary income falls off—prepare for retirement—or achieve any one of a hundred other wonderful things which lousy old money can do.

You may even forget how great and human a thing it is to help people own their own homes. There are a thousand technical things involved in the mortgage end of your business, and, here too, you may fail to see the forest for the trees.

Of course, financial advertising must have dignity, but that is no reason it should be deadly. Dignity can often be used as the easy way out. It is merely very lazy to be cagey and say little or nothing. But few of us are still impressed by the strong, silent man these days.

What has he behind that blank, immobile poker face?

George Bernard Shaw exaggerates this thought when he says: "Seriousness is only a small man's affectation of bigness."

The fairly uniform conventionality and drabness of the other fellow's advertising in the financial field offers to a lively outfit a wonderful opportunity to stand out with a touch of fun.

Just saying that you are a "friendly bank" is not enough. In fact, *that* has become almost a joke. Someday I'd like to get a bank to let me advertise it as "the unfriendly bank." I believe the humor of it, if presented well, would attract thousands of customers.

I even tried a piece of copy in this vein the other day—not with any serious idea that it would

be used, but just as an attempt to see if my idea could be even slightly approached.

We like people. We especially like people who do business with us. (We'd be ingrates if we didn't!)

Our courtesy and consideration for people is something we don't have for sale. It's just second nature for us to give it away. We are almost embarrassed to talk about it.

We wouldn't think of advertising ourselves as "the friendly bank." That would be almost like saying we are an "honest bank." Of course we are.

Nice people don't usually talk about how nice they are.

So, we are tempted to advertise ourselves as "the unfriendly bank" just to show our disdain for something we take as much for granted around here as we do our air-conditioning.

What we do want to talk about is our all-'round competent one-stop banking service—good, we think, in every department. Friendliness is too plentiful even to mention.

But if you want . . . etc.

Most financial institutions should break a bottle of the milk of human kindness on their doorsteps every morning.

Of couse it requires courage for a financial institution to do the unconventional thing in advertising. But this is true in all other fields of effort, even in invention and engineering. Charles F. Kettering once said: "We are prone to go by rules and rote, whereas all human progress must be outside the rules."

To those too timid to try humor in advertising, I would quote Dr. James B. Conant, who, when president of Harvard, had this motto on his wall: "Behold the turtle; he makes progress only when he sticks his neck out."

A man's best friend is his savings!

Is this true in your case? Because it *is* true that a Savings Account always stands by you, ready to help out in any emergency.

And at 94 convenient Chase Manhattan offices, your savings *get* help, too! Now **3%** interest each year, compounded and credited quarterly, on balances from $5 to $25,000.

Regular deposits benefit most from this big helping hand, of course. Open your Savings Account. Deposit $5 *today* ... and do it often! *Note: Deposits made by July 15th earn 3% from July 1st if left on deposit until the end of the quarter.*

THE CHASE MANHATTAN BANK
18 PINE STREET, NEW YORK 15, N. Y.
HAnover 2-6000, ext. 2401, N Dept. HT

I wish to open the type of Savings Account I've checked below. Please send me the necessary forms.

☐ INDIVIDUAL ACCOUNT   ☐ JOINT ACCOUNT   ☐ IN TRUST FOR

NAME _____

ADDRESS _____

_____
CITY   ZONE   STATE

THE CHASE MANHATTAN BANK

Member Federal Deposit Insurance Corporation

A stunning, humorous campaign by Chase Manhattan which was abandoned all too soon, probably because of the complaint of some crabby old lady stockholder or depositor. The childish grease-pencil technique by Howard Wilcox of Cunningham & Walsh, Inc., got this series, in newspaper ads and window posters, 10-fold attention, and won friends and influenced people by the very naïveté of treatment. Big corporations should have the courage of their originality in advertising, and should refuse to listen to self-appointed amateur kibitzers.

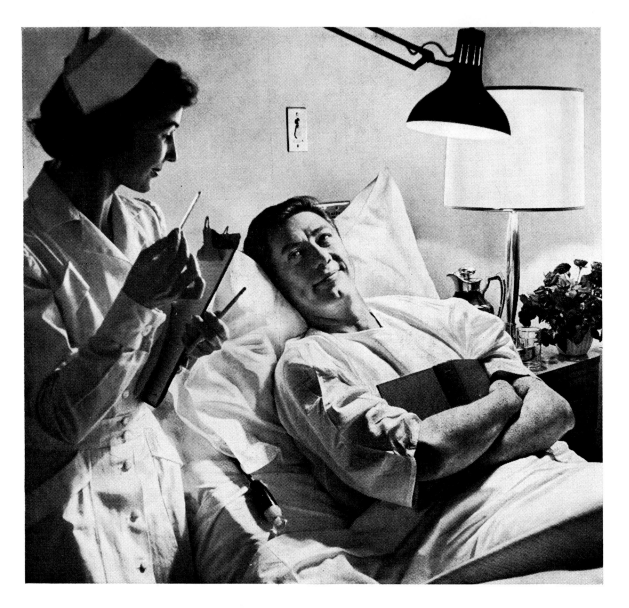

Nothing helps reduce a fever
like money in the bank

Worry never helped anybody get well.

Almost all of us get sick at one time or another, and when we do, one of the best medicines in the world is that secure feeling that there's enough money in the bank to pay the bills and run the house while we're getting well. The way to put that money there is to start saving, and the time to start is now. Come into The Bank and open an account as soon as you can, as little as one dollar will do it. But start now.

Write for our Save-by-Mail kit or phone us at FRanklin 2-6800, Extension 615. We're open Mondays from 9 a.m. to 8 p.m., and Tuesday through Friday from 9 a.m. to 2 p.m.

The Savings Department

 The First National Bank of Chicago

Dearborn, Monroe & Clark Streets · Building with Chicago since 1863

MEMBER FEDERAL DEPOSIT INSURANCE CORPORATION

This ad almost makes us wish we were sick in bed, with a dropping temperature, a pretty nurse and, who cares, maybe rising blood pressure. It adds up to a pleasant argument for saving money, and since First National of Chicago is so pleasant about the whole business, we might as well give *them* our business. (AGENCY: *Foote, Cone & Belding, Inc.*)

Why an oilman needs more than money from his banker

(a few refined words from Hubert, the Harris Lion)

"Far be it from me to sell a dollar short but it recently occurred to me that a lot more things than money are responsible for our many friends in the oil industry. Most of the oilmen we know could get a carload of cash somewhere else if they wanted to. But they don't. They keep coming back to Harris for a number of reasons.

"First off, they like to talk to banking men who understand their language. Here at Harris we know the difference between a 'Christmas Tree' and a catalyst.

"We also understand that an oilman is a combination explorer, producer, transporter, researcher, refiner, wholesaler, retailer—and each of these roles has its own dollar problems.

"I guess all the items we offer in addition to money add up to one thing: understanding your problems—financial and otherwise. We can't do anything about explaining your poker losses to the wife. But we can put our understanding to work for you as we have with other oilmen and their firms since petroleum first became a major U. S. industry.

"Write us, or, better yet, drop in and see us next time you're in Chicago."

HARRIS *Trust and Savings* BANK

Organized as N. W. Harris & Co. 1882—Incorporated 1907
115 WEST MONROE STREET, CHICAGO 90
Member Federal Reserve System...Federal Deposit Insurance Corporation

An appeal to a specific industry (oil) which appeals to all industries, in an ad by Leo Burnett Company, Inc., for Harris Trust and Savings Bank of Chicago. Leo Burnett has for many years been one of the, if not the, leading exponents of the light touch (for tough and tangible results) in many fields of American advertising.

Some years ago I pioneered the change from the old saying, "Save for a rainy day" to "Save for a sunny day." It makes much more cheerful reading and philosophy, and I've seen savings increase by leaps and bounds since it has been sold as being for fun, instead of as a grim, gruesome duty. *d.h.*

C. Douglas Wilson & Co. help you help yourself

by don herold

One good thing about a sensible mortgage loan on a home is that it is, yes, character building. It's stimulating!

It puts you on a track and helps you get the habit of saving money with regularity as you make the monthly payments.

Someone has said "Help from outside is often enfeebling, but help from within invariably invigorates." A C. Douglas Wlson & Co. loan helps you HELP YOURSELF.

"Mortgage" used to be a dirty word. Mortgages once came due all at once, and foreclosures were frequent and often villainous. But mortgages and mortgage lending have been humanized, so it is now easy to humanize mortgage loan advertising.

could you use a home improvement loan?

Is your house tired, rundown, losing its youthful beauty? Need a new roof? A paint job? An extra room? A Home Improvement Loan at The Atlantic will make your house look better fast—last longer, too. Drop in now and arrange for a low cost Home Improvement Loan.

Dogs are always sure-fire (along with babies, bathing beauties, mother, and the American flag). The dog appeal plus simplicity of layout and copy makes this home improvement loan ad for Atlantic National of Jacksonville quite captivating. (AGENCY: *Jacksonville Office of Wayne, Tucker, & Company*)

Thrift Talks   *by don herold*

Got an inbuilt hole in your pocket?

Then you'd better take the shortest walk to nearby National Savings. (It's no more than 6 minutes from anywhere in downtown New Haven.)

Some people, you know, just go through life, leaking money. It's so easy, unless you solder up the leak hole.

You have to have tricks for saving, since all the temptations are to spend. One trick is to save the TOP of every wad of money you get. Save first — then spend what's left.

Or hurry to the nearest mailbox with the top of your savings. Every U. S. mailbox is a "drive-up window" for National Savings.

National Savings will tempt you to keep up this habit by paying you good dividends on your savings.

current annual rate **4%** payable on 1st of Jan., Apr., July., Oct.

Deposits on or before the 10th draw interest from the 1st

Since everybody "hurts" with the way his income flows away like water, this ad should strike home with most readers. The first sentence ties in well with one of National Savings' themes—"No more than 6 minutes from anywhere in downtown New Haven."

127

"And I alone escaped to tell the tale..."

"There once was a holiday called the 4th of July and every year people were in such a hurry to enjoy this holiday that they jumped into their cars and rushed out to bump into other cars and turn each other over and run off of mountains and hit each other sideways until one year there were so many people in cars doing so many things they shouldn't have, that when the 4th of July was over and it was time for people to come back from the country and the mountains and the seashore there was nobody to come at all . . . . . and I discovered that I alone had lived to tell the tale!"

This 4th of July week end will be the longest in many years *THURSDAY TO MONDAY* which means that auto accidents will probably be the highest in many years . Care and courtesy <u>could</u> cut these accidents in half. Let's try.

THE TRAVELERS INSURANCE COMPANIES, Hartford, Connecticut.

The Travelers Insurance Company, The Travelers Indemnity Company, The Travelers Fire Insurance Company, Hartford, Connecticut.

This ad was written for Young & Rubicam and for Travelers by Doris Herold Lund, an improvement on the old block. Ran in *Editor & Publisher*, one year, just before the Fourth of July.

Would you be in the dog house if your house burned tonight?

by don herold

Last week I woke up to the fact that I was carrying only about 40% enough insurance on my house.

I'm the national average. The chances are you are, too.

We wouldn't think of roofing or painting only 40% of our house, yet the figures show that most of us go around with only one end of our houses insured. We may actually carry only enough insurance to protect the mortgage holder—nothing for ourselves.

IT'S WORSE TODAY

We always did carry too little insurance. And today we probably carry a heck of a lot too little, because replacement value of our homes has shot up (the national average of increase since 1939 is 45%), and we've let our insurance stand at pre-war levels. This is dila-

tory, darn-foolish and dangerous.

If your house burned tonight would you want only enough insurance money to rebuild only about two-fifths of it?

YOUR HOUSE IS WORTH MORE

Don't kid yourself about this discrepancy. Ask a contractor to give you a rough idea as to what he'd charge you to rebuild.

You'll get an answer which will probably shock you into upping your insurance as soon as you can fly to the phone and call an AMERICA FORE agent.

It is utterly ridiculous to carry too little insurance, because, in my opinion, fire insurance is one thing in this country that is dirt cheap today. (The average cost has gone down 40% in 30 years.)

What I say about home insurance

applies to furnishings, too.

BUSINESS PROPERTY, ALSO

Also to business property. Replacement values here, too, have skyrocketed in recent years but many owners are fast asleep with their same old pre-war insurance coverage. Ask your AMERICA FORE agent today to help you determine your real insurance needs —it's a technical problem which calls for expert help.

SEND FOR FREE BOOK

I've dug into this subject of today's new insurance needs and investigated new kinds of insurance available now, and I've written a little booklet about 'em which you can get by sending the coupon below. Among other things, this book helps you to make a simple inventory of your household possessions.

Reduction to absurdity is possible in humorous ads. How much better this dizzy diagrammatic treatment is than an "Is your house fully covered?" approach. Cartoons and crazy copy can often use the *reductio ad absurdum* technique to great advantage. (AGENCY: *Prince & Company, Inc.*)

Savings institutions are all handicapped by the prevalent propaganda that "There's no need to worry—Uncle Sam will take care of you" or, in some cases, "Your company pension will take care of you." It behooves savings institutions therefore to preach rather constantly, "Better look after yourself a little, too, just in case."

The home loan business is highly competitive among savings and loan associations, cooperative banks, mortgage bankers, savings banks, and commercial banks. If one of these institutions can add a touch of humor and cartoon charm to its advertising appeal, it has a competitive edge on others in the area.

A
SUBSTITUTE
FOR YOU

=

By Don Herold

A
Substitute
For You

By Don Herold

Most men think they have done swell by their families when they get their lives insured for a *round sum.*

"It will be nice for Mary and the children to get $50,000," they say. (Or some other round sum.)

The trouble with leaving a round sum is that the optimists immediately gather round. Mary's brother from Detroit appears with

3

Cover and first page of a successful series of six booklets addressed to fairly well-to-do prospects of the Trust Department of the Chase Manhattan Bank of New York.

HOW TO ENJOY YOUR MORTGAGE

You've started a wonderful adventure — that of owning your own home.

But the average person buys a home only once or twice in a lifetime and we find that a mortgage is something of a mystery to him. The purpose of this booklet is to help you understand your mortgage as the simple and friendly thing it really is. It will tell you a number of things you should know about your mortgage, so that you may live with it comfortably and happily.

Your mortgage will enable you to own more and more of your home each month, and thereby reduce your interest expense each month. (As your ownership see-saws up, your interest expense will see-saw down.)

- 1 -

A 16-page booklet published cooperatively by several savings and loan associations for distribution to home loan borrowers and prospects. It explains the pleasures of acquiring a home under the savings and loan plan of rent-like monthly payments including a part of the principal, the month's interest, and perhaps one-twelfth of the year's insurance and taxes. Also makes clear the advantages of prompt payments, the possibilities of saving interest by paying ahead at times, and other hints to borrowers and home owners.

Who's going to take care of me?
The answer is: your Second Income

children . . . or provide for travel or other types of fun which enrich life.

A second income could help take care of the expenses that pop up to surprise us all—arrival of children—teeth straightening, family illnesses—arrival of grandchildren (yes, Grandfather often pays for those, too), Aunt Lucy's fall downstairs, and other accidents and misfortunes.

Most of the good things of life come with saving and investing. They come with a second income. Ordinary day-to-day income may not be more than enough to just get by.

Of course, your circumstances may be such that it will be some time before you will need any kind of second income. But you can begin now to lay aside for it, and it will be a great satisfaction to you to help your second income fund grow.

Looking farther ahead, when your earning power may diminish and your first income may dwindle, a second income can become even more vitally important.

The way things are going, it's likely that even if you

4

have a company or personal pension, along with social security, it won't be enough to enable you to live *lively* when retirement years come.

Right now, millions of people who thought they would be comfortably fixed in later years have had to keep on working at something (if they are lucky enough to be able to) to round out even a fair living.

Inflation has always eventually occurred in America. Experts say we've had as much as an *average* of 3% inflation per year since 1900—which means that each year your money may have bought an average of 3% less. If this keeps up (and who can be sure it won't?), it could be bad for you 10 or 20 years or more from now.

A second income can be many times as good as just *one* income, because it's *plus*. It is only with a second income that *real* living starts for many people.

A second income could be the ice cream on your apple pie.

We don't want to "just live" —we want to plus live

5

Two pages from a 24-page booklet for Francis I. Du Pont & Co., investment brokers, entitled "Investing for a Second Income"—the general theme being that it's only with a second income that you really start living. The booklet explains how Francis I. Du Pont can help the reader make investments to help him acquire a second income in the simplest and most systematic way.

In line for another bathroom?

America has more bathrooms than any other country in the world. But one of our old customers said recently that, as far as he was concerned, America needed one more bathroom—in his house! If *you're* in line for a bathroom, garage, kitchen or other home improvement, we can help you. An FHA Home Improvement Loan from Iowa-Des Moines will bring the carpenters, plasterers and painters on the run! You can borrow any amount up to $3,500. If you borrow more than $600, take five years to repay. And you need not make a down payment. So don't stand in line a moment longer. Come right in or telephone us for the spot cash that will make yours a very much happier home.

We're here to help you get what you want **IOWA-DES MOINES** ✕ *National Bank*

Member Federal Deposit Insurance Corporation

Sixth and Walnut ▲ *CHerry 3-1191*

It's hard to get any drama or humor into advertising of home improvement loans. The Iowa-Des Moines National Bank has done a lovely job of capitalizing on the situation of the overcrowded family bathroom. What better, pleasanter way of implanting the idea of another bathroom with a loan from this good bank?

Shrunk

Money doesn't go so far today. With inflation, times have changed.
And so have your insurance needs. The value of your home, your furniture and other
personal possessions has soared sky high . . . about 70% in the last eight years for dwellings alone.
Why not play safe, financially? With the help of your Maryland agent or broker,
find out the actual replacement value of your home and all your furnishings and
personal effects at today's prices. Then bring your protection up to date.
Remember: *because your Maryland agent knows his business, it's good business for you to know him.*

MARYLAND CASUALTY COMPANY
Baltimore 3, Maryland

There are many forms of Maryland protection for business, industry, and the home. Casualty Insurance, Fidelity and Surety Bonds, and Fire and Marine Insurance are available through 10,000 agents and brokers.

Dramatic simplicity gives terrific impact to this Maryland Casualty ad. A dollar bill pinned to a clothes line! I can't imagine anybody skipping this or not liking Maryland Casualty better for thinking of it. (AGENCY: *J. M. Mathes, Incorporated*)

A railroad can be a grouch

Humor in Employee and Public Relations

Humor is of especial value in employee and public relations, because most companies, in both of these areas, grow self-conscious and frigid and produce something as grandiose as the President's Annual Report on the State of the Nation.

Here, more than in perhaps any other endeavor, a company should call on outside help, just as a surgeon summons another surgeon to operate on his own wife or child.

The outside medico is less apt to tremble or slip.

Again I must warn that I am not using the word humor to mean slapstick.

I want it here to mean freedom from starch or corporate stuffiness. Sometimes, companies, knowing their natural shortcomings, will even unknowingly tinge their messages to employees with a sense of guilt.

Almost invariably, the insider saturates the messages with swollen company ego.

And the most frequent handicap of corporations in these fields is the fear-imposed failure to say *anything*.

It's better to talk, talk, talk. Talk things over with employees. Explanation, even slightly fumbled, is better than stolid silence or any kind of dissemblance.

It is amazing how few know the value of forthright explanation in dealing with public or employees.

Most of the troubles that companies have with the public or with their own employees are due to a lack of simple explanation.

Any parent can learn the value of explanation from observing the reaction of kids. If we simply say "Do this!" or "Don't do that!" we get almost automatic resistance. But if we take the time and trouble to explain *why*, we can get almost anything we want from our offspring. They appreciate the appeal to their intelligence, and are flattered to be given credit for it.

Gimme those scissors, quick! NO!

Likewise, the public or a group of employees will respond to reason quietly put and free from bamboozling and bluster. Talk, to employees especially, must be gentle and diplomatic. Touches of humor can break down the "Oh yeahs!"

One thing I've noticed, too, is that talking over policies with the public or with employees often has the value of improving policies or establishing policies previously neglected. For example, several years ago I was asked to write an employee handbook for a large chemical company with 4,000 employees in the particular plant I was to cover. When I asked about their retirement plan I was told, "Well, when somebody here reaches retirement age and gets into trouble, we help out as best we can."

"How many people are you helping in that way now?"

"About thirty-five," I was informed.

"You have no retirement plan," I told them frankly, and explained what they'd have to have

to make a retirement plan worth writing about. Within a year or so, they had set up a real retirement plan, and I hope I had something to do with bringing it about.

we never like to see an employee leave

Many companies that spend hundreds of thousands of dollars for insurance and retirement plans seem reluctant to spend a few thousand more to cash in on the good will they could reap by telling their employees about their plans in simple language. Frequently they merely give them booklets prepared by insurance companies and these are almost invariably as clear as Sanskrit to the average reader.

It requires a bit of doing to translate these puzzlers into readable and inviting terms without violation of their real meaning. You have to produce almost a legal document, but with some lilt in it.

My first work in this field was for Johns-Manville. They felt that my kind of writing could be applied to a combined job of employee and public relations, and we started off with a series of plant-town newspaper ads in some seventeen cities in which J-M then had factories or mines, and this series ran every other week for several years. My efforts in these fields have been to make my messages anything but "institutional."

People simply don't know unless you tell 'em, and they won't listen at all if you ride a high horse.

You and The Reader's Digest

the green grass grows all around

we hope you like your job at the digest

You are now a member of a pretty large family—about 700 of us out here in the country the year 'round; sometimes twice that many during the pre-Christmas season, when we have millions of orders to fill for Christmas gift subscriptions. (This figure does not include nearly a hundred men and women in New York, doing editorial, art, and research work; nor, of course, does it include the hundreds who work in other countries at the offices of our 19 International Editions.)

We aim to keep this rather large establishment from becoming a mere machine in which personalities are lost. Others may think of the Digest as an "international whopper," but we want the feeling in the Digest offices to be that of a small-size, friendly organization. We are proud of our staff, and we hope every employee will take personal pride in his or her contribution, however large or small it may be.

We want the Reader's Digest to be one of the most pleasant of all places to work. To this end we try to pay salaries that compare favorably with those paid by others, to help you find the job here that suits you best, to be fair in our few rules and regulations, to be liberal in vacation provisions, and to give you assurance that you will have an income for your old age through our retirement income program.

5

Cover and page one of a handbook I created for employees of *The Reader's Digest*. While giving all the "rules and regulations," it tries to help create and maintain a family and small-town feeling with and among employees in the beautiful *Digest* "plant" at Chappaqua, N. Y.

Open car doors carefully

Two cars have nasty nicks as the result of gusty door handling by Mr. Hasty Parker in the above photo—his own car and his neighbor's.

Take a little care with car doors morning and night. (We're telling this, too, to the guy or gal parked next to you, to save YOUR CAR from bangs and dents.)

—The Digest

Don't be a canteen crum!

We're supposed to be a neat, civilized set of folks at The Digest—and most of us are. But we'd hate for a delegation of Digest readers to see what a mess some of us leave on the tables in the cafeteria —milk cartons, paper cups, spilled milk, coffee and other drinks, crumbs and other food!

And in the lounges, too!

There are refuse baskets in these rooms, and if each of us took just a couple of minutes to clear up his or her own clutter, how much better these places would look to—well, to us, ourselves.

—The Digest

No joking: no smoking, no choking

—— in buses for Reader's Digest employees.

This is serious.

Smoking in buses is impolite, inconsiderate and inexcusable.

Also it violates general public safety codes.

So, seriously, just don't smoke.

The Digest

Payroll enclosure slips used rather regularly to tell *Reader's Digest* employees pleasantly a few dos and don'ts to help keep life happy for all at the *Digest's* Chappaqua, N. Y., home.

A FAN LETTER TO B. & O. EMPLOYES about their Courtesy

by don herold

Dear B. & O. Employes—

I LIKE YOU men and women who are the Baltimore & Ohio Railroad, because you all seem to know that a railroad can be something more than steel rails and cars.

It can be rails and cars *and friendliness*.

"Rails and cars and courtesy" is how most folks would describe the B. & O.

But courtesy, in my opinion, is just another word for friendliness.

And you folks seem to have it more than any other big working group I've ever seen.

I don't know where you get it. Courtesy must be just plain "catching" among B. & O. employes.

Every time I've traveled on the B. & O. I've felt that I was a guest of everybody connected with the road—and not just 150 pounds of human freight that you had to get from New York to Chicago or somewhere.

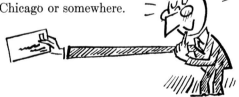

"Over-the-shoulder" technique used in a booklet on courtesy for the B. & O. employees, with the expectation that if thousands of the booklets are "left lying around," B. & O. patrons, also, would sneak a look at them. (AGENCY: *The Richard A. Foley Advertising Agency, Inc.* [*now Bayer, Trip-Foley, Inc.*])

"Going Steady" Is Nice With Jobs, Too

You'll have to ask a lot of people before you find one who won't agree that a good steady job — is a pretty good thing. Because you can't turn off your living expenses during a lay-off.

And that's one reason so many Gardner people find Heywood-Wakefield a good place to work. We have our ups and downs, to be sure. But, we make a sincere — and pretty successful — effort to keep up a steady pace.

It's not easy, nor entirely due to luck in times like these, either. It helps, of course, that our business representing many different products is not especially seasonal in nature.

But a very important reason why we have been able to keep our people on the payroll so regularly is this. We have tried to keep a sensible reserve to tide us over periods when we actually have to spend more to keep going than we take in.

HEYWOOD-WAKEFIELD
H·W
EST. 1826

A good way to reach employees and, at the same time, thousands of "fellow citizens," is with plant-town ads in local newspapers. Here are two of a series done for Heywood-Wakefield of Gardner, Mass., produced in cooperation with the Charles W. Hoyt Company, Inc.

No Sign On The President's Door!

People who drop in to see the president of Heywood-Wakefield don't find the usual sign, "President" or "private" on his office door. For the simple reason that his office has no door to hang a sign on!

There's a rumor that the office of the president he worked for had a door — but it's no rumor that it was always open, So, when the office space was done over last time, it seemed silly to bother with a door that was never closed.

Like any business that's been at the same stand for 121 years, Heywood-Wakefield has some traditions. One of them is the open door to the president's office.

It means he's as much a part of the picture as the chap at the next bench — and no harder to talk to. And that is one of the things people like about working at Heywood-Wakefield.

Should Business Conventions Be No Fun?

There are those who think that business conventions should be held in old warehouses or abandoned street-car barns.

They forget that a convention, when held at a delightful place like Ponte Vedra (on the ocean between Jacksonville and St. Augustine), can provide an ideally quiet place for concentration at intense business sessions, but a place which also offers health, mental refreshment, morale improvement, a new start in life —and yes, let's offer the dirty word—*fun.*

The thought of applying austerity to gatherings of representatives of a business organization is foreign to American thinking.

So, bring your convention to Ponte Vedra or to any of America's outstanding resort hotels to relax and to concentrate. You'll go home more fit to increase your company and personal earnings, and thus put both in a higher tax bracket for the glory of the Internal Revenue Service.

Ponte Vedra offers everything in one spot—perfect accommodations for conventions up to 250, the ocean at one door of The Inn, golf at the other, tennis, a surf club, dancing, sunning, sleep and general all 'round re-invigoration for the over-strained American business man and tax producer.

Ponte Vedra

THE INN · THE GOLF CLUB · THE SURF CLUB
Ponte Vedra Beach, Florida

*ANYWAY... send for a seductive
Ponte Vedra Convention folder.*

One afternoon when I arrived at the Ponte Vedra Inn in Ponte Vedra Beach, Florida, I found the management concerned about the rising discussion of opposition by the government to company convention expenditures at better-class resort hotels. The next morning I suggested this bit of back talk, and by 9:30 A.M., we had copy on its way to *The Wall Street Journal* and to Washington, D. C., newspapers. —*d.h.*

OF FRIENDSHIP

A talk to employees of Knott Hotels about courtesy

WRITTEN FOR KNOTT HOTELS

by don herold

(A TYPICAL GUEST)

Maybe things are bad at home—somebody sick or in trouble. It's noble not to show **that** to the guests. (And certainly no hotel employee should ever spill his troubles to a guest.)

You Are the Hotel

One thing to remember always is that YOU ARE THE HOTEL to the guest to whom you are talking or whom you are helping.

If you're pleasant, the hotel is pleasant. If you're grouchy, it's a lousy hotel.

No business in the world is as dependent on its employees as a hotel in this matter of public impression.

((4))

Another "over-the-shoulder" book addressed to employees, but with the idea that hotel guests, too, would get the feeling of Knott Hotels' sincere concern for good treatment of guests. Perhaps part of the joy that guests found in reading it was the pleasure that often comes with "eavesdropping."

Even If Courtesy Didn't Pay

by don herold

Why should anyone be courteous? One answer is, it pays—but there are better answers than that.

It's more fun.

It saves wear and tear.

If an organization is keyed to courtesy, it's more of a pleasure to work in that organization. And there's less friction and fatigue in working in such an organization. Days are smoother and happier. You go home less beaten and bushed.

Courtesy makes life—everyday life—an art, instead of a chore.

I'm not preaching. I don't care whether you're courteous or not—except to me. I'm just thinking out loud for my own good. Am I, myself, going to be courteous—or not?

Yes, I'm going to try to be courteous,

morning, I find I feel like barking at other people, myself, all day. One short, crispy, discourteous crack out of *anybody* and I'm inclined to be a little grumpy inside all day. Oh, it will be subconscious—but there'll be something poisonous gnawing at me for many hours.

On the other hand, if somebody goes out of his way to *take time* to show courtesy to me, I'm apt to be goofy nice to everybody else the rest of the day!

The point is, courtesy and discourtesy are so doggoned catching!

That's why courtesy is so important in an organization, in a company, in an office. It spreads so easily. So why not start spreadin'?

Notice I said "take time" in a para-

because I'll get more kick out of life and because I'll probably live longer.

I've noticed that it doesn't take much *dis*courtesy from somebody else to muddy up a day for me.

If somebody barks at me on the telephone or in an office or store early in the

graph above?

Courtesy is half a matter of common sense and human kindness—and half a matter of taking a little time. I'll take time to go into that in another article.

Meantime, try courtesy and see if it kills you. It may *cure* you.

Two good media for messages to employees are house organ columns and payroll slip-ins. Here are examples of the former for Crown Cork & Seal, and one of a series of the latter for Texaco.

Railroads are not built—
they are rebuilt!

➜ Even though the Baltimore & Ohio Railroad *is* 118 years old, it is *always new*. Today, you'd have a hard time finding a speck of the original B&O anywhere, except in its spirit of service and its old-fashioned courtesy. Physically, it is continuously rebuilding itself in every detail—replacing and improving—becoming more modern by the hour.

Every year, for example, hundreds of miles of new steel rails and millions of new cross-ties become a part of B&O's 11,000 miles of track. New and more efficient steam and diesel locomotives, as well as passenger and freight cars, replace faithful, retiring "old timers". By adding here, replacing there, B&O keeps its service constantly as modern as today.

This unending job of building is your assurance that the B&O continues to bring to you and your community, *as always*, the finest in progress-making rail service.

Baltimore & Ohio Railroad

The public doesn't know unless you tell 'em. Most any company is missing a bet unless it tells the world some of the behind-the-scenes sweat and sweetness of its business. Here are two "talk-to-the-people" ads for newspapers in towns reached by the Baltimore & Ohio. (AGENCY: *The Richard A. Foley Advertising Agency, Inc.* [*now Bayer, Trip-Foley, Inc.*])

HOURS AND PAY
(Two Pretty Important Things)

Making a chemical product is often like baking a cake. You can't walk off and leave it in the oven. When you have started it, you have to "keep baking."

So, many of our processes are continuous. They can't be interrupted. We can't stop them halfway. They must go on 24 hours a day, 7 days a week. Some of our products are "in the oven" as long as three weeks.

And many of you in the plant (not in the offices) must therefore work on different shifts, so we can keep up this uninterrupted process. We discuss this with you when you first come to work, and try to have a clear understanding about it.

many chemical processes are relay jobs

This "continuous production" is one of the main reasons why we have to have pretty good teamwork between you and the other fellow. When you are ready to go home, you don't want the next fellow to be late to take your place. And vice versa. And you don't want him to be absent without notifying the plant. It's fair to everybody for everybody to stick to schedules.

Normally, you'll work 8 hours a day, 5 days a week—total 40 hours. But during busy times we have to increase them, and when we do, you'll be paid extra. Work schedules are posted each week for the next week. Ask your Supervisor about your schedule.

Pay—When and How

Our rates of pay are in line with or above rates in our surrounding area. They are based on a system of measuring "job worth" which is unusual and, we believe, very fair.

The modern way to pay you is by check. Then if you lose it, you haven't really lost it. You can get another.

6

Cover and page 6 of a 40-page book telling the many thousands of employees of Calco Chemical the facts and fun of life at the Calco plant at Boundbrook, N. J. Most important of all is that many chemical processes are continuous, 24 hours a day, up to 3 weeks in flow, and that this calls for prompt arrival on the shift or notification of absence in advance. Page 6 spells this out.

It's nice to work with a successful company

1957 WAS PENNEY'S BEST YEAR—SALES ALMOST 1⅓rd BILLION

It was a BANNER YEAR

by don herold

EDITOR'S NOTE—*Don Herold is widely known for his knack of making complicated subjects easy to understand. He is the author of many articles and books on a variety of subjects and his pithy observations are often quoted in The Reader's Digest and other publications. He has been a regular PENNEY NEWS contributor for many years.*

It's comfortable to work for a company that makes a *habit* of success.

Penney's has made a profit in each of its 56 years (except one—1920) and it has paid dividends continually since its beginning.

And every one of Penney's associates is glad of it! It seems to me that each Penney year is at least a *little better* than the last. At any rate, last year was the best yet in Penney history, with sales of $1,312,278,407.77, and net earnings of $49,410,892, at a new high of $6.00 a share. (Dividends were $4.25 a share.)

No Roller-Coaster Flights and Drops

Some companies have a tough time all the time, and just manage to get along. Other companies have high years and low years—exciting, maybe, but not very conducive to peace of mind.

I'd say: "Gimme a sound, steady grower like Penney's, and I'll stay for life."

"We Start From Here"

I hear and record the Penney story every year, but, no matter how good it is, there is never any note of satisfied smugness in the Company's reports. Every year-end is more a year-beginning than a year-end, at Penney's.

A DOOZY of a December

December, 1957 was the best month Penney's ever had. Sales for that month ($202,376,464) were greater than sales for the entire year of 1933. This good December came at a time when many other companies were wondering what was happening.

HIGH-QUALITY MERCHANDISE

COMPETENT PLEASANT SALESPERSON

+ = PLEASED CUSTOMER

THE PENNEY SUCCESS FORMULA IN A CAPSULE

Multiply this by millions and you have Penney's

---

are in the quality of its merchandise and its people. It does not sell seconds, irregulars or sub-standard merchandise. And when it comes to people, it does not employ "seconds, irregulars or sub-standards."

VERY SIMPLE— Each Sales Person Pleases Each Customer

The 1,694 Penney stores are not merely 1,694 buildings. They are groups of warm, cooperative, well-trained associates, who know that good retailing depends largely on how well the individual salesperson pleases the individual customer. Penney's is millions and millions of individual sales satisfying millions and millions of individual customers.

Penney personnel-customer relations were improved even more than ever in 1957 by advancing progress in recruiting and training associates. And the Penney policy of sharing profits

"During the last quarter of 1957," wrote Penney President A. W. Hughes, "there was a change in the economic climate in our country. The year ended in an atmosphere of doubt and hesitation."

Let 'Er Rip— Penney's Is Prepared

So Penney's hitched its galluses up for a greater effort than ever in 1958.

Aw, I wouldn't want to work for any company that made a profit.

Never fear—you won't

President Hughes felt sure, for many reasons, that Penney's will weather any weather the future may bring. Here are some of 'em:

(1) Penney's sells daily needs and wants. (People are more likely than ever to come to Penney's when they want to economize.)

(2) There's the Company's record since 1902. (Everything has happened to the country in those 56 years and Penney's has grown through thick and thin.)

(3) The Company's strong and liquid financial position. (Available cash and short-term government securities at the close of 1957 totaled $153,395,332; and inventories amounted to $185,576,375.)

(4) Penney's 1,694 stores are broadly scattered in 48 states.

(5) Then there's the nation-wide, long-time recognition of the quality and value of Penney merchandise.

(6) And, of course, there are the ripe experience and staunch morale of Penney people.

Penney's knows that its success and future promise

surely adds an eagerness to individual efforts which customers do not find in many businesses.

And the constant improvement of the Penney profit-sharing retirement plan counts positively, too. (There'll be a lot in coming issues of PENNEY NEWS about the new Penco PROFIT-SHARING Retirement Plan. Watch for news on this.)

26 New Stores— Making 1,694

The store story tells the whole Penney story to some extent. There were 1,694 stores at the end of 1957. In 1957, the Company opened 26 new stores in 19 different states. 23 of the stores were in suburban shopping centers.

In addition, 35 existing stores were relocated in new buildings, and 19 small stores were closed. 145 other stores were improved, enlarged or refixtured. (It is not true that Penney's is out to close all its stores in small communities. No Penney store will be closed where a careful survey reveals there is an opportunity for increased volume.)

About 19 new stores are definitely scheduled for 1958.

Penney's and Credit

Last year the Company told its stockholders that it intended to test credit sales in a small group of stores. A lot of people then started saying that Penney's has "gone to a credit policy." The test has not even yet been started, and when it is, it will be tried in only a limited area. That's the beauty of an outfit with 1,694 separate branches. You can try things on a small scale before you make sweeping changes.

A Toast to Associates and Suppliers

To me, an outsider, but a friendly, close observer of Penney's, this Company seems to me to be a model for free enterprise the world over. It lets its associates alone as much as possible (would that all governments were as good at *that!*) It gives 'em responsibility and then lays off. With the exception of about 50 stores, Penney's leases its stores and lets its landlords make money. It fosters the long-time cooperation of thousands of suppliers and lets

1958 may be a little stormy. So what!

PENNEY'S

them make money. It gives bonuses to store managers and individual salespersons and lets them make better money for greater individual effort.

"Without our people and without our suppliers, where would we be!" exclaims President Hughes at the end of every year. Customers by the millions naturally follow.

Taxes As Usual— Or More So

Of course, as heretofore, the Company worked more for the government than for itself. Taxes totaled about $53 million (against payments to shareholders for use of their money (dividends) of $4.25 a share. Taxes took $8.08 a share.

We welcome opportunities and problems ahead

Once a year for many years, J. C. Penney has rendered a financial report to its employees on the back page of its employees' publication, "Penney News." This is slanted to employees, written in simple terms (as even stockholder reports should be, but mostly aren't) and pointing out what the facts presented mean particularly to Penney workers. The report is distributed later in inexpensive booklet form.

J-M Smokestack
By Jim Asbestos

What if there were no factories in the world?

Shucks! We could start one in a week or so—shucks!

Let's Imagine—No Factories

Sometimes we may get a little mad at factories, and think we'd be better off without them.

But, just for fun, let's imagine that tomorrow morning we'd get up and there'd be no factories in the world.

Those of us who want jobs would have to scramble fast. Maybe 10,000 of us would meet in a vacant field on the edge of town and decide to start a factory to give us jobs.

What would we make? It has taken most factories fom 10 to 50 years to figure that out—to perfect their products. Johns-Manville, for instance, now has several hundred men who do nothing but figure up J-M products for 1, 5, 10 years from now.

We'd need a building and we'd need machinery and raw materials—maybe $10,000's worth per man. This would call for 100 million dollars. We haven't got 'em. We'd have to get some backers— some thrifty folks, maybe 10,000 of them —to put up the 100 million. We would be willing to pay them a reasonable rent on their money (dividends). They'd be taking a risk; it's no more than fair that they should be rewarded for taking a chance on us.

We'd need smart managers to run our factory. We'd find other groups bidding for the managers. We'd have to pay these men good salaries.

We'd have to send salesmen out to sell our products. (Johns-Manville has several hundred such salesmen.)

Maybe in five years we'd be ready to roll.

Starting a factory is no bed of roses, so—before we decide we'd be better off without the factory we work for, let's imagine 10,000 of us in a vacant field deciding to start one of our own tomorrow morning.

—Jim Asbestos

JOHNS-MANVILLE

"Talk it over" is a policy that always pays any company in its relations with the public and with its employees. Too many corporations still play it poker-faced with both groups, or wait too long to start talking. It was several years ago that Johns-Manville asked me to write this biweekly column for all towns in which they had plants, and they kept the columns going consistently for several years. The columns were signed by "Jim Asbestos," a typical J-M employee. The same messages worked all right for both employees and the public. Incidentally, the columns did a job, too, of selling free competitive enterprise to everybody. (It would help if more companies found opportunities to get in a good word here and there now and then for the system which has made their growth possible.) —d.h.

It happened in White Oak, Maryland. A robin decided to build her nest in the shelter of a public phone booth. To give her peace and quiet, local Bell Telephone men (of The Chesapeake & Potomac Telephone Companies) quickly installed another phone on a nearby phone pole. Result: service as usual, mother and family (four) doing very well. (And thousands of new friends for A. T. & T.) The photo and story were later featured by Bell in a full-page ad in national magazines. (Photo by *The Evening Star,* Washington, D. C.)

Public relations? Well, at least broadly educational. This is a book on the benefits of Vitamin C prepared for the Florida Citrus Commission for wide distribution in public schools. Its preparation involved research in the New York Public Library on the really scientific measures taken by doctors in the British navy about 200 years ago to determine the effects of citrus fruits in preventing scurvy on British ships. The booklet was written and illustrated with cartoons, to interest children in good old Vitamin C.

Humor in Direct Mail

Genius is 98 per cent directness.
—WALT WHITMAN

I like direct mail advertising because it can be so direct.

In many cases you can call your shots with almost deadly accuracy—that is, be certain you're aiming at somebody who is pretty sure to be interested.

This invariably inspires better writing.

Some years ago when I worked in big "shops," I frequently felt prostituted because 90 per cent of everything everybody wrote was destined for the wastebasket. I mean, if I were one of ten people assigned to write the same ad, I felt something like a street walker. I wanted to be *the* guy assigned to write *the* ad.

Not that I don't believe in wastebaskets.

The greatest trouble with a lot of direct mail is that it looks too much like direct mail.

It has a slick, overdone, overperfect, professional finish, with perhaps too many colors, which marks it as factory-made direct mail, and gets it assigned promptly to the outgoing trash.

It was the overproduction of such stuff that caused Abe Martin (Kin Hubbard) to write: "Lafe Bud found a real letter in his mail yesterday."

I like direct mail to have a casual appearance, to suggest, almost, that it has been thought up on the spur of the moment. A relaxed look will inspire relaxed acceptance, whereas overprepared messages look too calculated.

A touch of humor will add to the effect of ease, even if it goes so far as to seem almost amateurish, and it will appear to suggest easy reading.

One thing I like about direct mail is that it gives a writer room to tell everything.

Said C. A. Bethge:

Direct mail copy should be long enough to answer every question that might come into the buyer's mind.

A fault of a great bulk of direct mail advertising, to my mind, is that it doesn't tell enough. I believe in long letters, that the more you tell, the more you sell. If the merchandise is right—that of course is the first essential upon which direct mail advertising must rest—you have an interesting story to tell; and if you want your mailing piece to sell, you must give the prospect the whole of that story.

You've seen throughout this book that I am somewhat prejudiced against "hit and run" advertising. I like a complete performance, where possible, and direct mail offers this opportunity.

I'd rather advertise thoroughly to one man than superficially to ten.

When you need more than an honest face

An honest face won't get you any-place when you're fresh out of cash in a strange town.

It won't get you a decent meal, a good night's sleep, plane fare home, or a clean shirt.

Carte Blanche will get you all these things—and many more.

You can even have slightly shifty eyes from watching tennis matches, and Carte Blanche will still work famously.

Carte Blanche membership auto-matically ranks you among the solid financial citizenry. This pays off in red-carpet treatment from more than 100,000 fine establishments. It also pays off with the documentation you need under the new tax law.

Carte Blanche is the credit card that carries more weight. Nice thing to have even though people frequently mistake you for Perry Mason.

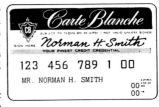

THE CREDIT CARD THAT CARRIES MORE WEIGHT

Please see reverse side for listing of charge services

Happy direct-mail piece from Carte Blanche, which sells hard by selling soft.

One of a series of dizzily delightful bulletins sent frequently to customers and prospects by Fortnum & Mason, famous, frolicsome London grocers. They call them "Commentaries."

One of a series of four cartoon folders supplied by Strathmore Paper to paper dealers, with dealer imprints on page 2.

Another in the series of four cartoon mailers supplied by Strathmore Paper to its dealers.

GLUYAS
WILLIAMS

launched his new Product on the market and saw it gain headway. The new merchandising scheme was a Natural. The Product wowed the populace at first sight. Bixby hired a crew of hail-fellows-well-met and sent them on the road to Jolly the Dealers and keep them happy until production could catch up with demand.

Bixby always believed that, when you had a Light, the silliest thing to do with it was to Hide it under a Bushel. So

BIXBY soon became a household word. His name was on every lip.

Bixby was on the billboards. Bixby was in all the best newspapers. Bixby was in the morning mail. Bixby was on a major network, coast to coast. Bixby was in magazines and rotogravure, in four colours. Advertising agencies scrambled for the Bixby account. The Bixby product almost exhausted the copy writers' stocks of four-dollar adjectives. It was that <u>Good</u>!

A page from a whacking fine book, *Bixby's Dilemma*, size 10¼″ × 13¾″, for The E. B. Eddy Co. Ltd., Fine Papers Division, made entrancing by beautiful cartoon illustrations by Gluyas Williams, master of all advertising cartoonists. (ARTIST'S REPRESENTATIVE: *Kennedy Associaties, Inc., New York City*)

You wouldn't wear bathing suits like these

— yet possibly your eyeglasses are just as outdated

IT'S FUNNY how quickly styles change, and convert serious modes of today into laughs of tomorrow.

This season's hat may be a riot in six months and today's skirt length may be a scream by this time next year.

Cover and introductory page of a booklet I did for the Better Vision Institute, for distribution by optical-dealer members. An effort to ridicule old-fashioned eyeglass frames, and to establish the fact that eyeglass fashions change and become ridiculous as definitely as fashions in clothes. —d.h.

Dear Subscriber:
I have been looking everywhere for the renewal of your FORTUNE subscription.

So short that you are moved to renew your *Fortune* subscription, in gratitude to them for sparing you the mayhem to which many magazines subject you if you don't resubscribe instantly.

HOW THE EDISON VOICEWRITER GROWS ON YOU

by don herold

Most people who try dictating machines are annoyed at first by the new experience of talking to an inanimate object. Sometimes they're even paralyzed and struck dumb. To meet this trouble half way, Edison Voicewriter had me write this book telling my own initial annoyance at using their dictating machine, and my ultimate complete enjoyment in using the appliance. They gave copies to prospects testing the machine and to new buyers of the Voicewriter. I was in a good position to give solace to new users. —d.h. (AGENCY: *J. Walter Thompson Company*)

This is silly — talking to an inanimate object

I'd almost rather give up Mrs. Herold than give *it* up.

The most ardent dictating machine user I know told me frankly, "I'd as soon have faced a firing squad as face that machine at first. But today, it's practically an extension of my mind and larynx. At first it was stultifying; now it's stimulating. I use it in my car, have one at my bedside at home, and I telephone to it from three or four spots in my factory."

It's a Little Mental Problem at First

Anybody can learn to operate an Edison Voicewriter mechanically in almost a few minutes. Physically, you can certainly feel at home with it in a couple of days.

But, psychologically, you may have a minor tussle with it that will last a little longer. Just regard this as normal — and worth while, and don't take it seriously. It

2

HOW TO CHOOSE A POCKET SLIDE RULE
by Don Herold

Copyright 1951 by Keuffel & Esser Co.

As Your Constant Bosom Companion
by Don Herold

This is an age of portability. "Take it with you" is the slogan of the day.

You slide rule users are behind the times if you aren't carrying a concentrated, boiled-down, slide rule with you 24 hours a day.

You ought to see the little pocket editions that K&E is making. Your fingers will itch to work 'em. In their neat little sheaths they are hardly any bigger than a pocket comb.

Every engineer, scientist, business man and student who ever needs a slide rule, should immediately annex one of these babies, to use whenever and wherever the slide rule impulse hits him.

You wouldn't tote a grandfather clock when you can carry a wrist watch

Cover and two pages from a 12-page folder selling Keuffel & Esser pocket slide rules.

162

Don't be a slave to your husband's shirts

DEAR MRS. WIFE:

You can use your mind and your muscles in much better ways than in washing and ironing your husband's shirts.

You wouldn't churn butter. Well, doing a shirt at home is just as old-fashioned as churning butter.

Most women agree that a good professional laundry like ours can do a better job on men's shirts than they, and the cost is so little that it's one of the best buys a housewife can make.

We have special equipment and supplies and expert help that enable us to do a wonderful job on shirts.

Among our supplies is Velvet Rainbow, which gives shirts a fine full body, combined with smooth pliability. This keeps a shirt comfortable, smart-looking and fresh all day and evening.

Switch to us for a try on your husband's shirts -- and we believe you'll have a happier life and a snappier-looking husband.

Sincerely,

Manager's Signature

Manager
YOUR NAME LAUNDRY

YOUR NAME LAUNDRY

YOUR ADDRESS

YOUR TELEPHONE

An inexpensive one-color letter supplied by Velvet Rainbow to laundries to persuade more housewives to escape household slavery by sending their husband's shirts to laundries for professional handling. (AGENCY: *Chirurg & Cairns, Inc.*)

Any man feels superior in a shirt done by this professional laundry

DEAR MRS. WIFE:

I won't say a well-laundered shirt will bring a man success.

But success often hinges on small things, and I know a smart-looking shirt makes me feel just a little bit superior. It makes me feel I have just a little edge on the other guys.

And maybe that edge is exactly what your man needs when he goes to work in the morning.

Women are wonderful, but personally I know (and my wife admits) that our professional laundry can do shirts better than she can.

Mrs. Herold says it's partly because our laundry uses Velvet Rainbow, which isn't even on sale at retail stores.

Anyway, I'm not keen about having my wife spending her time over a hot shirt. Laundry costs are so reasonable and results are so wonderful.

In your town, I recommend the laundry whose name is over there in the corner. Just try sending your husband's shirts to them and only to them.

Phone them today.

Sincerely,

Don Herold

for
NAME OF LAUNDRY

YOUR NAME LAUNDRY

YOUR ADDRESS

YOUR TELEPHONE

Another letter supplied by Velvet Rainbow to professional laundries to send to housewives. This one has the possible added value of being signed by a third-person, shirt-wearing husband. (AGENCY: *Chirurg & Cairns, Inc.*)

One of a series of cartoon post cards, supplied by Texaco to its dealers for neighborhood mailing. These had advertising only on the address side. Nothing but fun on the message side. This is what you might call subduing the commercial.

Two pages of a 14-page accordion folder for the nearly 50,000 door-to-door subscription salesmen of *The Reader's Digest*.

The Knox plan REQUIRES no drugs, no calorie counting, no starvation— and a minimum of character

No Penitentiary Routine

The best thing about the KNOX EAT-AND-REDUCE PLAN is that it treats you like a human being. It doesn't put you in jail or in a straight-jacket.

And while it reduces you, The Plan sets you up with a practical, nutritionally balanced diet program for a lifetime of pleasing slimness.

When you follow The Knox Plan you are sure of getting your daily requirements of:

- *proteins* • *vitamins*
- *minerals* • *bulk*
- *proper proportion of liquid to solid fats*

It even provides for three "sneak snacks" a day to brace you up and help you escape hunger discomfort.

2

do you really want to lose weight?

then here's the KNOX EAT AND REDUCE PLAN

A booklet I did for Knox gelatin, taking off from the recognized hardships of most reducing plans—starvation, calorie counting, drugs and use of one's character. Elbert Hubbard used to say, "Get them walking down the street with you in the opening paragraphs." (AGENCY: *Charles W. Hoyt Company, Inc.*)

First page of a hard-boiled, four-page illustrated letter to hard-boiled truck tire prospects. Inside shows photos of trucks on tough construction jobs.

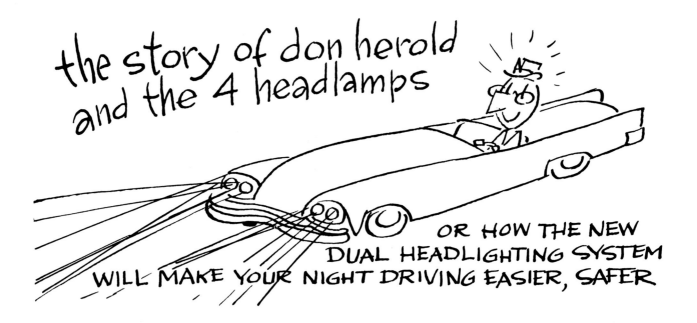

the story of don herold and the 4 headlamps

OR HOW THE NEW DUAL HEADLIGHTING SYSTEM WILL MAKE YOUR NIGHT DRIVING EASIER, SAFER

I'm all lit up!

by don herold

IF YOU THINK those 4 headlights on the new cars are put there just to look cute, guess again.

I, myself, thought they were put on merely to fancy up the front of the car—until I, myself, bought a new car with 4 headlights.

Before I got 'em I figured I had been getting home at night all right on two—headlamps, that is.

It didn't take me long to learn that these twin lights on each side of my car are the greatest advancement in car lighting—the finest aids to safe, pleasant night driving—

A wide-swinging horizontal book for Tung-Sol Electric, Inc. to sell their Dual Vision-Aid head lamps. There is a whole little booklet describing the advantages of this type of headlight, and Tung-Sol believed in not hiding these advantages under a bushel, but in educating the public about them. (AGENCY: *E. M. Freystadt Associates, Inc.*)

ᵀellevision

ʿnow the
ʿessional
ʿness.
EBERG

porarily as stores) and make our evenings hideous with their repeated blasts about bad breath, irregularity, upset stomach, B. O., sinus pains, and headaches that hammer the hell out of us.

This is an ag   ved
by persistent irr.

It is the essenc
ing gains in world
disputes. It is even   ʿ-
the Senate. And oʿ
technique of childreʿ
parents down.

And, alas, it is emplo
sion advertisers who beʿ
public into buying their

George Washington Hʿ
Tobacco Company was perʿ
greatest exponent of the neʿ
shamelessly admitted his belieʿ
public with repetitious shoutinʿ   ,
for example, "L.S.M.F.T." (Lucʿ   ʿ Means
Fine Tobacco), and "Lucky Stʿke green has
gone to war." (For some reason or other, the
green ink on the packages was needed at the
front lines.) Lucky are those of you young enough
to have missed this plague.

But today there are more and more raucous
pitchmen who come into our living rooms (which
we have graciously permitted them to use tem-

I am for countering this deliberate use of premeditated sales violence and vulgarity by organizing sensitive blocks of the public who will blacklist a lot of products off the shelves of corner stores. I still won't buy Lucky Strikes as my personal answer to George Washington Hill, even though he is now long in his grave.

The vulgarities I deplore and the endless repetition and the shouting are all of course totally lacking in humor and are therefore worth discussion in a book entitled *Humor in Advertising.*

The most articulate and most persuasive advocate of deliberate irritation and all-'round pragmatic cussedness in advertising today is Rosser Reeves.

He summarizes his case against creative people and all measure of good taste with his story of the advertising magazine that "asked the creative people of twenty-five top agencies to name the three worst TV commercials of the past several years. Of the three commercials these men and women picked, two were the most dramatically successful commercials of the past twenty years. One had introduced a new product, and in just 18 months had swept aside all competition. The second commercial, in another field, had done almost the same thing."

What would Mr. Reeves recommend? That every agency maintain a stable of sensitive, creative people in cribs (as on the old Barbary Coast in San Francisco), take a poll of them on each proposed campaign, and cross off those campaigns approved by the stable? This would put the best minds of advertising right smack into the oldest profession in the world.

All right, let's say the two worst commercials mentioned above brought a fast buck to the happy manufacturers of those two products.

What, meantime, were they doing to advertising in general, and perhaps to the long-term destiny of the two products themselves?

I am aware of a mightily growing distaste for offensive advertising, both print and broadcast. I see too much walking to the kitchen and to the bathroom during TV commercials, when I am in homes where there are television sets. I hear too many people saying "Nuts!" to the blandishments of airway pitchmen. I now see too many blab-offs on television sets. (These are small contra-receptive devices costing about $5 which anybody can buy to shut off crummy commercials.)

So what of the future of television if Mr. Reeves' gospel prevails? And of all advertising, because television can drag print advertising down with it (and a lot of print advertising is creating its own quagmire).

Let's listen to a typical housewife, Lois Green Howard, of Connecticut:

I've heard someone say "Tell your mommy to buy it" once too often. . . .

Although I was interested in the product at first, my irritation at the repetition soon put an end to my interest.

I don't buy products whose commercials are broadcast louder than the rest of the regular program.

How would we react if we went into a grocery store and found that certain displays were wired to yell at us to gain our attention?

Many advertising men themselves believe today that commercials are ruining television. *Tide* (later absorbed by *Printers' Ink*) had a 2,200 Leadership Panel which it surveyed on this subject, and it made a report on the findings, which called spades spades. The words most used by *Tide*'s panel members in their reports were: "too brassy," "phony," "wild and restless," "detestable," "smug." One panelist said that "the commercials may get attention, but so does a toothache."

But sometimes the bruisers can present figures and cite situations which seem to prove that crudity pays and that good taste, restraint, and humor don't get across. I always take their proofs with a big grain of salt.

The cause of humor in advertising was set back temporarily by the regrettable withdrawal of Bert and Harry for Piels beer, which I regarded as perhaps the best example of lighthearted commercials of all time. Yet, all of a sudden, Piels discontinued them because they were not increasing the volume of Piels sales.

I talked to a number of people who said that they loved Bert and Harry and had tried to support them, but could not stand the beer. Piels at that time must really have been a lousy beer, for their very next campaign said: "Look what's happened to Piels!" And, thinking they must have been shooting at a too-highbrow audience with Bert and Harry, Piels next used commercials with photos of bulbous-nosed roughnecks—commercials obviously aimed at a mass lowbrow audience instead of a "class" market.

Bert and Harry were the brain children of Ed Graham, then of Young & Rubicam, and were designed by Jack Sidebotham, head of Young & Rubicam's art department. The voices were those of Bob Elliott and Ray Goulding.

When Piels changed to a huskier flavor, they should have retained the good will built up for the beer by Bert and Harry and used them to announce an improvement in the beer instead of firing them and going to lowbrow commercials.

Bert and Harry fans raised such a hullabaloo about their disappearance that Piels finally decided, after two years, that they had made a big mistake in killing them off, and brought them back with great fanfare.

This is the first and only case in history that I know of the public demanding the return of any type of radio or television commercial.

Piels published "An Open Letter from Bert and Harry Piel" and ran an ad purporting to be a news item to the effect that their advertising director had accepted a challenge to debate Bert and Harry.

Of course they were restored, and I hope Piels beer is now good enough to live up to Bert and Harry.

Here's a sample of Bert and Harry conversation, good because it came at a time when there was a lot of talk about the need for restraint of advertising claims. Harry, always the braggart, makes outlandish claims for Piels, while Bert, at his elbow, tries persistently to tone him down.

HARRY: I'm Harry Piel. You know, it's no accident that Piels beer has a reputation for "fresh-poured flavor."
BERT: Er, wait a minute, Harry. Er, yeah, that's all right.

HARRY: Just pour a glass of today's Piels and you'll notice its long-lasting head. . . .
BERT: Er, probably.
HARRY: Now that's a big reason why Piels tastes extra good.
BERT: Many agree.
HARRY: The long-lasting head acts like a seal up there. . . .
BERT: Er, virtually.
HARRY: . . . keeping flavor and freshness from escaping.
BERT: We certainly hope . . . heh.
HARRY: And that's why Piels fresh-poured flavor lasts all the way down.
BERT: Many impartial people have stated that.
HARRY: Why do you keep qualifying everything I say, Bert?
BERT: Well, no exaggerated advertising claims for us. I'm taming down your pitch.
HARRY: But why? Every word was true.
BERT: Look, Harry. . . . An honest, ordinary description of Piels beer sounds like an exaggeration. If I'd never tasted it, I'd assume you were talking through your hat . . . figuratively speaking.
HARRY: Well, if that's true, everyone who hasn't, please try today's Piels immediately, and then you'll know I'm not exaggerating.
BERT: Most likely.
HARRY: Oh, now, Bert. . . .
BERT: All right—definitely!

Ballantine commercials have been pretty good and quite amusing and very tuneful through the years, and their beer has been good, and their sales have steadily climbed.

I often think that advertisers could learn something from the results of two contrasting techniques used by two of Queen Victoria's prime ministers. It has been said that Gladstone got on poorly with Victoria and that Disraeli got on very well with her, because Gladstone addressed her as if she were a public meeting whereas Disraeli talked to her as if she were a woman.

"When I first spoke on the radio, David Sarnoff, president of the Radio Corporation of America, gave me some good advice," said Dorothy Thompson: 'Always remember that the microphone is not a megaphone. It is an ear. Do not speak to millions. Speak to one person, and remember that person is sitting right across the table from you. It is his ear to which you are speaking—not the nation.' "

If a salesman in a store talked to me as many of these television fellows do, I'd slap his face and walk out of the store. Imagine a salesman shouting at me like that, pointing his finger at me, hammering at me, or fawning on me so fulsomely.

As someone has said, it's too great a price to pay for free movies.

One thing I simply cannot understand in television advertising is the fondness some sponsors have for putting their messages in the mouths of half-witted adults and little idiot children. This is the worst misuse of so-called humor that advertising indulges in today.

Take that moron plumber, for example, who sells Dash. Who wants advice from a palpable ignoramus like him? (No offense to the guy who is playing the part, but the advertiser makes him talk like Mortimer Snerd.)

Personally I've always been annoyed by the little Alka Seltzer pest, Speedy. Also, it was a great relief to me when that horrible little Johnnie, the bellboy who cried "Call for Philip Morris," was abandoned, I hope forever.

Some of these characters have no doubt moved merchandise, but I wonder how much more the manufacturers could have sold if they had not chosen to *sell by torture*.

One of the unhappiest bits of cleverness I can remember in TV is the Simoniz commercial that featured Peter Lorre cleaning a hearse.

Some of the many things that drive me wild in television are (and they all indicate a lack of a sense of humor in sponsors and producers):

Split speeches, where two different people read alternate sentences of the sponsor's message. (Imagine two salesmen working on you like that in a store.)

Messages yelled into a rain barrel to increase the volume.

Hopped-up applause of the commercials themselves by instructed TV audiences.

The repeated use of the summarizing sing-song "Yes," and the frequently interjected "You see." Of course I see.

The "yum, yum, yum" of food salesmen. "Um-m-m, man *that's* coffee!"

Announcers answering "Right!" when somebody has stated the merits of a product.

Commercials shouted excitedly at double speed to give us an effect of cataclysmic importance.

Says Stan Freberg, president, Freberg, Ltd.: "The woman listener has been beaten about the ears with the baseball bat of hard sell, or what is worse to me, dull sell, for so long now that it is a little hard to get a message through the scar tissue."

John Crosby once suggested a soap commercial: "It gets the dirt off. It doesn't make you twenty years younger, it won't win you a husband (or wife), it won't patch up a busted romance, but it gets the dirt off."

Crosby tells of a broadcasting old-timer, Charles H. Crutchfield, then an announcer at WBT in Charlotte, North Carolina, who ignored the radio air audience in his commercials, selected a man from the studio audience, sat him down opposite him at a table, and talked to *him*.

Crosby calls Arthur Godfrey possibly the greatest debunker of stuffy commercials on the air. Godfrey told Crosby of an experience he'd had when he was a disc jockey in Baltimore. Godfrey was reading a commercial in which a store advertised $50 and $60 suits for $17.50. Midway through the commercial, Godfrey got disgusted and said: "Hey, wait a minute! This sounds like a lot of hooey. I'll go around and see this guy and let you know about the suits tomorrow."

He did just that. The next day he explained to his listeners that the store was selling $30 suits, not $50 and $60 suits, for $17.50 and that the storekeeper was a nice fellow. That commercial cleaned out the store and Godfrey has been a firm believer in telling the truth ever since.

Truth, humor—same thing.

Perhaps the most consistently humorous commercials through the years have been those of Jack Benny.

Here is an excerpt from one of Benny's commercials for Jell-O desserts (General Foods Corporation):

Jack has Peter Lorre on the show. After a song by another guest artist:

JACK: That was beautiful. . . . (Jack turns to Peter.) Now Peter, I'm sure that even you will have to admit that she sings much better than you do.

PETER: Do you really think so? (Takes out switchblade kinfe.)

JACK: Peter, put away that knife. I'm going to tell you something . . . you and that knife of yours. Ever since you've been rehearsing for this show I haven't been myself. I've been a nervous wreck.

(Cut to Don Wilson as he enters with man.)

DON: Oh, Jack . . . Jack.

JACK: Excuse me a minute, Peter. (Jack goes over to Don.) What is it, Don?

DON: Well, we found the man to publicize Jell-O gelatin dessert, and we flew him all the way from Manchester, New Hampshire.

JACK: That's wonderful, Don. I didn't think it was possible. Go ahead, sir . . . tell the people your name.

MAN: My name is Mr. E. B. Jell-O.

JACK: How about that . . . his name is Jell-O.

DON: And you spell it the way we do, don't you?

MAN: Oh, yes. (Sings.) J-E-L-L-O.

JACK: You don't have to sing it. . . .

DON: You must be proud being named after such a famous product as new Jell-O.

MAN: Yes, I'm proud of being named after a dessert that now has that fresh fruit taste in all twelve flavors, including their two new flavors, mixed fruit and lemon-lime. And by the way, Mr. Benny, I want to thank you for bringing my wife and family all the way to California.

JACK: Oh, you brought your family with you?

MAN: That's right. I brought all four kids—Strawberry, Raspberry, Cherry and Irving.

JACK: Wait a minute. With a last name like Jell-O I can understand Strawberry, Raspberry, and Cherry, but why did you call one of them Irving?

MAN: Well, I thought we should name one after my father.

JACK: Oh, your father was Irving Jell-O?

MAN: No, Fred Irving.

JACK: Wait a minute. If your father's last name is Irving, then your last name should be Irving.

MAN: It was, but I changed it to Jell-O.

JACK: Why?

MAN: How else could I get you to fly my whole family clear across the country?

JACK: What?

MAN: We're having a wonderful vacation.

JACK: Get out of here.

MAN: Tomorrow we're going to Disneyland.

JACK: You won't be here tomorrow. Don, get this chiseler on the first bus out of here. And I'll settle with you later.

Lois Green Howard, our Connecticut housewife, declared: "When Bob Hope says 'It may be dessert to you, but it's bread and butter to me,' I listen."

And Bob sells Beechnut gum when he says: "I've been using Beechnut gum for twenty-five years. Its price has never changed. It is either a big bargain now, or it was a big gyp then."

Alfred Hitchcock has made commercials more effective by poking fun at them. "According to statistics, a murder will be committed during the next sixty seconds—as well as four armed robberies, thirty-three petty thefts, and a forgery. There will also be a television commercial. If you doubt me, watch."

After a Young & Rubicam-produced commercial, Hitchcock said: "For those of you who failed to grasp the point of that message, it was prepared by my sponsor, who wishes you to buy his product. I don't think that's an unreasonable request to make."

Still another: "Oh, dear, I see the actors won't be ready for another sixty seconds. However, thanks to our sponsor's remarkable foresight, we have a message that will fit in here nicely." I understand that much of the credit for the Hitchcock commercials goes to Jim Allerdice of Revue Productions, formerly a writer for George Gobel.

Ed Graham, of Bert and Harry fame, was responsible for another delightful cartoon character in commercials, Emily Tipp (voice by Margaret Hamilton) for Tiptop Bread.

One I used to like was Parker Fennelly's Titus Patch for Pepperidge Farm Bread.

Some of the most delightful commercials being done in the year I wrote this (and I hope forever) are those old-movie commercials for Seven-Up, (J. Walter Thompson Company, Chicago; Sarra Studios). They are pure, captivating absurdity. For example, an old-time rushing mob of thousands approaching the camera—"When friends drop in unexpectedly, give them Seven-Up."

Or: "Having trouble with that new lawn?"

"The favorite drink of all suburbanites is crystal-clean, sparkling Seven-Up."

Or: "When the crab grass gets ahead of you. . . ."

"Enjoy the real thirst-quencher, Seven-Up."

Seven-Up has also made beautiful use of cartoons by George Clark (J. Walter Thompson Company, Chicago; Ansel-Sarra Studios), and other cartoonists.

Here's part of a George Clark commercial, for example:

The audio runs:

'Hi. . . . my name is Eloise Britton of Appleton, Wisconsin, creator of the Approved Eloise Britton of Appleton, Wisconsin Method of Making Telephone Calls to Friends. Step One: Take chilled bottle of Seven-Up from refrigerator for when your throat gets so dry from talking. If you don't have some Seven-Up to quench your thirst . . . you'll *die!* . . . I mean, *really*. Also take a little snack—some meat, cheese, pickles, mustard—you know. Of course if you plan on talking for over two and a half hours, get an extra Seven-Up. Step Two: Spread out on floor sprawl-like—next to phone, and you're ready! Crazy!

Sparkling Seven-Up is the real thirst quencher. That fresh, clean taste—exclusively, uniquely Seven-Up—makes any food a positive feast."

The happiest TV audio dialogue of all time was this excerpt from a Midus Muffler commercial:
"You have a noisy muffler."
"I can't hear you. I have a noisy muffler."

As a part-time Florida resident I enjoy the line of a television cartoon Southern Colonel who, in advertising Southern Bread, expresses the ultimate endorsement: "I'd go North for Southern Bread."

So, you see it *is* possible for fun to bring home the bacon in television commercials.

I am convinced of the ultimate doom of grim and gauche commercials. Captive audiences are not as captive as you think.

The escape? Pay-TV? Stan Freberg says not. "It won't succeed. People won't pay to hate something they can hate for nothing."

Alan Barzman of Klein/Barzman, advertising consultants of Los Angeles, lists these as two of the outstanding overworked commercial formats:

1. The "Get the Girl—Get the Guy" commercial. This suggests that you can win the lady by putting a particular brand of car wax on your auto; make out like a tall dog if you dab this hair cream on your head.

2. The "Aren't We All Having Fun Here at the Backyard Barbecue or Down at the Beach or in the Party Room Because Mom's Just Brought in a Platter of Our Product So Why Not Let's All Gather Round the Piano and Break into Song About It" commercial.

One of the few TV commercial announcers I rush home to catch is Barbara Feldon for Revlon, on the Ed Sullivan show. I leave cocktail and other parties early to be sure not to miss her. She kids all serious cosmetic salesladies so delightfully that I'm sure she'll sell millions of barrels of Revlon lotions and sprays. Fact is, I enjoy her commercials more than any of the regular acts on the Sullivan show, and I'm tempted to reward her humor with lavish purchases for my lady friend, Mrs. Herold.

An Open Letter from Bert and Harry Piel

Mr. E. Gordon Gibbs
Director of Advertising
Piel Bros.
Brooklyn and Staten Island, N. Y.
Sir:

Two years ago you stood in front of a Piels directors' meeting and said that Harry and I weren't doing a very good job selling Piels Beer. You told them that our kind of flamboyant personal selling went out with straw trolley car seats. To sell beer today, Piels must use today's advanced scientific methods of mass persuasion. In short, you said Harry and I were old-fashioned.

I suppose, E. Gordon Gibbs, if we'd known you better, we wouldn't have been so shocked. There you were, an efficiency expert hired by us two months before, challenging my brother and me, with sixty years between us in the business. You had our jobs to gain and nothing to lose. Well, Harry and I didn't even bother to speak up then, we were so sure that the directors would spot you for a phony. But they didn't, and we were out and you

were in, and that was that.

That was two years ago. Now we're speaking up.

Now We Challenge You To A Public Debate

Maybe Harry and I were old-fashioned. We talked to our viewers as friends. We respected their good sense and good taste. We didn't show any diagrams of congested nasal passages at dinner time, if that's what you mean by modern selling.

We want to debate the issue, your way or our way, with the people as judges. Anywhere, anytime you like.

There will be another Piels directors' meeting in October. And this time Harry and I are not going to keep silent. We're going to try and get our jobs back. The directors will want to know what the people say.

Are you willing to hear the people speak, E. Gordon Gibbs?

Bert Piel
Harry Piel

When Piel Bros. could no longer resist public pressure to bring back their television characters, Bert and Harry, their agency, Young & Rubicam, created a fictitious personage (an efficiency expert named E. Gordon Gibbs) on whom they placed the onus of Bert and Harry's dismissal, and staged a public debate to test the popularity of Bert and Harry. Over 3 million ballots were submitted and Bert and Harry were reinstated after two years' absence, and E. Gordon Gibbs was offered a job at Piels counting bottle tops. (He is now probably working for Brand X.)

Humor Helps Posters

There's no better place for humor than in posters, where the reader is on the run and the message must be quick.

"Plant a smile and it'll last a mile," and give the prospect the chance to enjoy his own wisdom in grasping it so quickly.

"Make a funny" and you'll make a friend—goes for posters. You've caught the motorist (or pedestrian) in a happy mood, ready to become happier, and with a mind pretty surely open for a merry message. Even if the humor is slightly cryptic, he'll enjoy chewing on it down the street or highway.

Savignac, great French poster artist, has said: "Essentially, the poster must see things simply. Posters must use the language of childhood—the universal language. All people are children. They enjoy the viewpoint of children. But this does not exclude subtlety."

For Savignac, subtlety is achieved through the use of humor. "Humor," he says, "is essential, because modern man does not have many opportunities to laugh. Humor is the antidote to the harsh realities of life." As noted earlier in this book, humor increases acceptability of life, of advertising, and of the product advertised.

"Art directors seem in agreement that humorous treatment is increasing in the outdoor medium," says W. F. Flower, vice-president and director of public relations of Outdoor Advertising Incorporated. "It is especially interesting to note that most of these humorous posters are top prize winners."

What motorist hasn't had his trip made more enjoyable by the roadside jingles of Burma-Shave?

Since 1926, up to 7,000 sets of these have been planted nationwide by the Burma-Vita Company of Minneapolis, six to a set, spaced about a hundred feet apart, along the country's main highways.

Here are a few you may remember:

We've made grandpa
Look so youthful
His pension board
Thinks
He's untruthful.
Burma-Shave

Another:

Use our cream
And we betcha
Girls won't wait
They'll come
And getcha.
Burma-Shave

Sometimes Burma-Shave merely preaches a little roadside safety sermon, such as:

Don't take
A curve
At 60 per
We hate to lose
A customer.
Burma-Shave

One secret of *bad* poster design is set down by John Amon, art director of Needham, Louis and Brorby, Inc., Chicago, an agency exceptionally good at poster designs: "In too many instances, the artist or art director is not allowed to run around loose. Almost invariably someone tells him what to do and how to do it. The result is technically good, contrived and safe. But it generally lacks imagination."

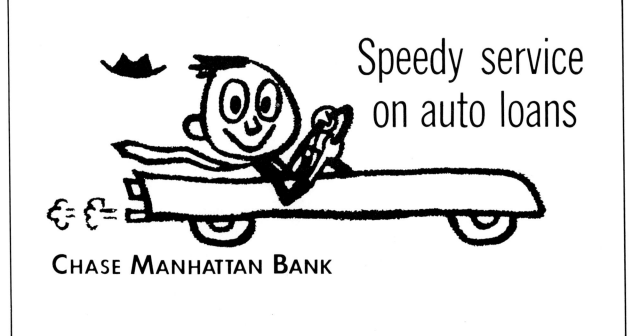

Window cards in childish grease-pencil technique, harmonizing with newspaper ads at the time—for Chase Manhattan Bank. Really inspired treatment by Howard Wilcox, art director of one of the bank's agencies, Cunningham & Walsh, Inc.

Ford won a First Grand Award in 1954 on this one. (AGENCY: *J. Walter Thompson Company*; ARTIST: *Scott Johnston*)

Dogs again! Another totally endearing poster for Ford by Scott Johnston. (AGENCY: *J. Walter Thompson Company*)

For almost three decades, Wrigley's gum has charmed America with the lovely posters by Otis Shepard—always happy, always in impeccable good taste. These have appeared not only on the highways, but as car and bus cards and in television commercials.

Be sure wiht Pure

Lovely nonsense in a billboard. Much more appealing and rememberable than some solemn message about octane rating or other obscure technical advantages of "pure oil." (AGENCY: *Leo Burnett Company, Inc.*)

Even when grim, humor serves its purpose, and when you are selling safe driving, you are going direct to your market when you use roadside billboards like this one for the Madison County Mutual Automobile Insurance Company of Edwardsville, Ill. (*Created by Everhart Signs.*)

THE YANKEES ARE COMING!

Motorists up and down Route U. S. 301 and on Route U. S. 501 get cumulative fun (and selling) out of a series of consistently snappy and always colorful billboards for about 100 miles north and 100 miles south, promoting one of the country's most successful motels, "South of the Border," near Dillon, S. C.

Some of these may be audacious to the point of offending a few persnickity prospective patrons, but they have attracted millions of customers, and "South of the Border" now has 150 rooms, two swimming pools, two busy restaurants, a big gas and service station, a thriving gift shop, and solid booking through the winter months.

"South of the Border" was founded in 1951 by Allan Schafer, and it has had a phenomenal growth, thanks to its lively billboards, and to its good, comfortable accommodations. Menus and gift-shop display cards all talk in the same fresh patois of Pedro—the motel's mythical mouthpiece. "The Yankees are coming! Man the cash registers!"

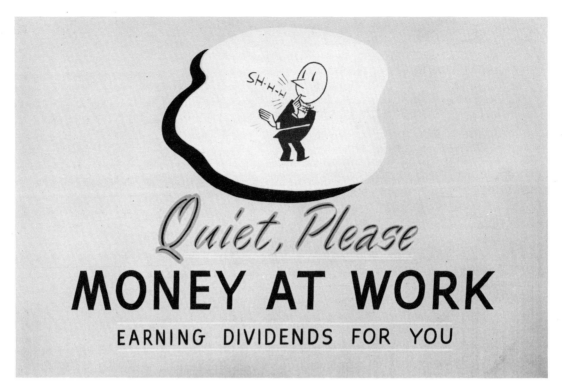

A lobby poster for several savings and loan associations stolen frankly (and adapted) from a sign on the Lucky Strike factory at Richmond, where it referred to tobacco sleeping and aging. —d.h.

Another lobby poster for several savings and loan associations, meeting the perhaps growing expectancy of many people to be "taken care of" by "someone."

For once, a legitimate use of the stone-age, no-forehead moron, in a fun-stunning poster for the *Chicago Tribune*. (AGENCY: *Foote, Cone & Belding, Inc.;* ARTIST: *Ed Renfro*)

Refreshingly simple childish 24-sheet and back-bar signs for the Dixie Brewing Co., New Orleans. (AGENCY: *Fitzgerald Advertising Agency, Inc.*)

Eloquence in seven words on behalf of the Yellow Pages. Fostered by Pacific Northwest Bell, Seattle. (AGENCY: *Guild, Bascom & Bonfigli, Inc.*)

Even when you're going 70 miles an hour, this poster will make you feel you're being passed by a better car. Fantastic suggestion of speed.

Here's another instance of picking your prospects with a rifle, by using roadside billboards. Many's the time we've all been tired enough on a long tour to be wide open to the suggestion: "Next time try the *train*."

Terrifically effective use of double-barrelled twin billboards to sell Mrs. Wagner's apple pie. (Designed by George Elliott of *Smith Greenland Company, Inc., New York Branch of General Outdoor Advertising Co., Inc.*)

Indians would make good copywriters for posters. Here's one who has really been put to work for the outdoor advertising industry.

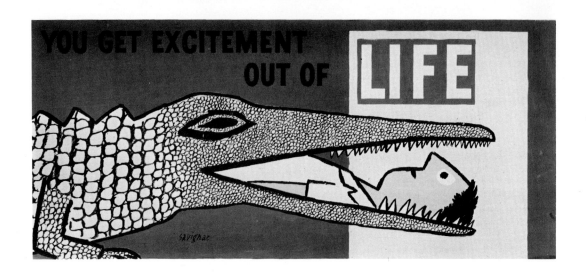

Three fun posters for *Life* magazine by famous French poster designer, Savignac. (*Outdoor Advertising Association of America.*)

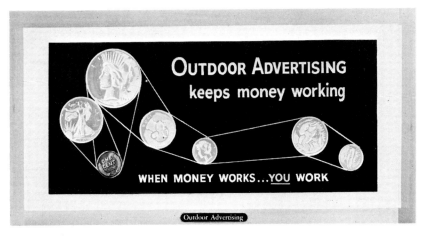

These posters were displayed throughout the country by members of the Outdoor Advertising Association of America in a campaign to familiarize the public with the role of the outdoor medium in the nation's economy. O.A.A.A's 700 members are operators of outdoor advertising facilities in 15,000 cities and towns.

A poster with red-hot sales appeal to anybody who has tried to beat summer heat in a back-yard department-store swimming pool. Sure to sell GE air conditioners.

Maybe this book is going to the dogs, but here's another ribbon winner, with his dinner—Ken-L-Ration. (AGENCY: *Needham, Louis and Brorby, Inc.*)

Again, naïve, childish art proves its bewitchcraft. (AGENCY: *Needham, Louis and Brorby, Inc.*; ARTISTS: *Frank Johnson and John Howard*)

Craz-eee!

There have been examples of success in advertising which has gone clear overboard in humorous and exaggerated frankness.

For example, in Burlington, Iowa, Harold Lyons reported no decrease in box-office receipts after he advertised on his marquee: "Two Features—Neither Is Any Good."

Another movie exhibitor advertised in the Jasper, Tennessee, *Journal:* "Cross Roads Drive-In Theater. Friday: *And God Created Woman,* with Brigitte Bardot. In color. Not recommended for children, teen-agers—or adults."

Walter Winchell reports a sign in a New York antique shop window: "Oddities, Antiques and Monstrosities." And a poster over the mirror in a Third Avenue bar: "If You're Drinking To Forget, Kindly Pay in Advance."

Another amusing sign in a liquor establishment is reported by *The Reader's Digest.* In a Chicago package store a poster reads:

Since you cannot refrain from drinking, why not start a saloon in your own home? Be the only customer and you will not have to buy a license. Give your wife $55 to buy a case of whiskey. There are 240 drinks in a case. Buy all your drinks from your wife at 60 cents a drink and in 12 days (when the case is gone) your wife will have $89 to put in the bank and $55 to buy another case. If you live ten years and continue to buy all your whiskey from your wife and then die in your boots, your widow will have $27,085.47 on deposit. . . . enough to bring up your children, pay off the mortgage on the house, marry a decent man and forget she ever knew a bum like you."

William B. Stout successfully promoted several projects with his shocking frankness a few years ago.

"I should like a thousand dollars—and I can only promise you one thing; you'll never see it again." With this sales talk, young Stout financed the first thick-wing metal airplane. People who bought this stock later realized four for one on their money.

"Invest with me and lose your shirt" was the line with which Stout financed another company.

George Tucker reports the ingratiating forthrightness of a woman selling gardenias outside the Music Hall in New York.

"I am not starving and I do not have 17 children to feed," ran her sales chatter. "I sell flowers because I love flowers and enjoy selling them. If you care to buy, they are 25 cents each, and I will thank you. If you are not interested, that is your business, and God speed you on your way."

She emptied five baskets in fifteen minutes.

"This is Dull—but Important" is the line that heads a golf club ad in *Punch.* That's somewhat irresistible, isn't it? The English are behind us in layouts, but sometimes miles ahead of us on copy.

"Buy these cars and save my life," read the headline of an ad by a Miami used-car dealer, R. S. Evans. You may bet he got a lot of readers and made a lot of sales.

Back in 1909 Henry Ford decreed that perfection had been attained and that henceforth there would be only one car—the Model T, or "Tin Lizzie." The vogue for calling them Tin Lizzies was encouraged by Ford himself, against the earnest advice of his executives. An old lady was supposed to have sent the company a barrelful of tin cans. By return mail she was said to have received a Model T and a letter from Henry Ford himself saying that a few cans had been left over and would be credited to her account. It did not matter to Ford how silly the stories were as long as Ford became a household word.

The Equitable Trust Company in New York once wanted to distribute a booklet. They ran ads with the headline: "Any Man Can Get Along Without This Book . . . but Not Without the Knowledge It Contains." Their supply of booklets was exhausted in a few days.

The almost self-deprecating technique has been used successfully in television commercials by several advertisers. Notable among them is the California Oil Company's Chevron Gas, which has used a nutty salesman, Hy Finn, as their spokesman. (Created by Batten, Barton, Durstine & Osborn, Inc.; account executive, Ed Wetzel; advertising manager, Max Barry.)

Here are some of Hy Finn's delightful lines:

A tankful of Chevron Supreme will last for years . . . if you don't drive.

With Chevron Supreme gasoline you can back up as well as go forward.

This stuff is great. They ought to advertise it.

In every gallon of Chevron Supreme there are four quarts.

Chevron Supreme is so good, even the dealers use it.

Chevron ran a contest and offered $75 worth of gasoline as prizes, with "Win enough gas to drive you to distraction!"

It is said that Chevron sales increased at a substantially greater rate than the average for the petroleum industry.

In Sherman, Texas, a department store printed an advertisement offering regular $2 shirts for $3. Sold out.

In London, an honest farmer inserted this personal advertisement in a Sunday newspaper: "Wanted—a wife with tractor. Send photo of tractor."

In Portland, Oregon, Robert Kuhn advertised in the *Oregon Journal:* "Veteran, wife, 10 dogs, 3 female cats, alligator, desire small furn. apt. We drink, smoke, stay up all night beating kettle-drums." He got twenty-five offers.

An irate mother traveling with her baby posted a notice in the washroom of a Rock Island railroad train asking: "Will the party who pilfered my baby's pants please meet me in the club car to match and see whether I get the pants or she gets the baby?"

The culprit returned the diapers to the mother who had left them in the washroom.

Typical radio commercial of Little Bennie, who is doing a land-office business in two gas stations in Oklahoma City:

Even if I had a model T Ford I wouldn't let Little Bennie service it. . . . In the first place, I've heard that he waters the gasoline until it will hardly fire at all. . . . I'm telling you Little Bennie will hook you every chance he gets. . . . If you should ever drive in there, watch out for your tires. . . . Bennie keeps glass and tacks all over the driveway so you'll have a puncture or blow out . . .

I recently heard of a successful use of humor in advertising by two college boys hitchhiking north from Miami after a spring vacation.

They held up a card, "Returning to Princeton." No invitations to ride.

They decided to be less serious with "Just a Couple of Bums." No invitations.

Then desperation brought inspiration, with "We give S. & H. Green Stamps," and they got an immediate invitation to ride north.

The most effective real estate salesman in London, Roy Brooks, has built his business on such weekly ads as this:

Seedy family house, two rooms in basement. Decor peeling, faded, floral and flyblown. If you are too late to secure this gem, we have a spare along the road, rather more derelict. A lightly built member of our staff negotiated the basement stair but our Mr. Halstead went crashing through.

Compensation for Attention

The use of valid humor in advertising somewhat repays the reader for listening to your selfish attack on his purse. (I know: you are really telling him something for his own good, something to his economic advantage, but, just the same, he deserves a lump of sugar for pausing.)

Let's face it, you are after his money. So, basically, advertising is, after all, a pretty presumptuous proposition—asking the other fellow to sit still while you extract his dollars. We ought to be pretty nice about it. We ought to be pretty humble about it. We ought, somehow, to make our reader glad we are frisking him.

An Ad Is a Person

I feel that every time we advertisers create an advertisement we should stop to ask ourselves what kind of person it would be if it were a person.

Would it be dry and solemn and too hell-bent on selling? Would it be bombastic? Would its talk have the ring of the set speech of a doorbell ringer?

Or would it be genial, easy-going, sincere, confident enough of the goodness of its goods not to get inflamed about them, and with an undercurrent of the saving grace of humor?

Why Isn't There More?

Why isn't there more *good* humor in advertising?

Because the hardest thing in the world to control is abandon.

Because it is easier for uninspired workers to depend on IBM machines and grim logic than to achieve results with the curve of a little finger.

At this point I'd like to set down a favorite quotation of mine from G. K. Chesterton in his book, *Orthodoxy:*

The bird can of its nature go upwards, because fragility is force. In perfect force there is a kind of frivolity, an airiness that can maintain itself in the air. Modern investigators of miraculous history have solemnly admitted that a characteristic of the great saints is their power of "levitation." They might go further; a characteristic of the great saints is their power of levity. Angels can fly because they take themselves lightly.

. . . One "settles down" into a sort of selfish seriousness; but one has to rise to a gay self-forgetfulness. A man "falls" into a brown study; he reaches up at a blue sky. Seriousness is not a virtue. It would be a heresy, but a much more sensible heresy to say that *seriousness is a vice.* It is really a natural trend or lapse into taking one's self gravely, because it is the easiest thing to do. It is much easier to write a good *Times* leading article than a good joke for *Punch.* For solemnity flows out of men naturally; but laughter is a leap. It is easy to be heavy; hard to be light. Satan fell by the force of gravity.

And while I'm quoting, there's Oscar Wilde's: "It is a curious fact that people are never so trivial as when they take themselves very seriously."

Among the pitfalls, the advertiser may make

the mistake of using a humorist who knows nothing about selling, or of trying to make a humorist out of a sales-trained advertising writer.

The client himself, who may have no sense of humor and little sense of daring, is apt to clobber a humorous campaign by the exercise of an overcautious and insensitive blue pencil.

There are a hundred practitioners of advertising who can exert meticulous carefulness and who can exert relentless will power, for each one who is gifted with creative ability. It's all right for one of the former to watch the latter, but not too hard.

"I would like to suggest to management everywhere an annual Let-Creative-People-Alone-Week," says Herb Mayes.

Humor in Advertising
Can Save $Billions

Humor in advertising is so effective that it makes most other techniques in advertising look extravagant.

Certainly not all products nor all subjects lend themselves to its use.

But any advertiser should ask the question: Can I use humor to advantage? If he can, he can save a lot of money. I feel sorry for him if he can't. I also feel sorry for him if he tries to use humor and becomes ridiculous and unbelievable.

Strange as it seems, I invariably approach skeptically the use of light-vein copy and of cartoons. I have to sell myself or be sold on the appropriateness of employing them in individual cases. I definitely approach every assignment with a study of the down-to-earth serious things

that are to be said. In the early stages of doing a new job, I am as concerned and as dedicated as a surgeon.

I want to know I am on solid ground before I kick up my heels.

Humor in advertising looks easy, but it may be extremely difficult. Take cartoons: I may spend three hours and draw twenty cartoons of a certain subject, the same subject, none of which satisfies me, and then spend fifteen minutes "undrawing" my subject, and get what I want.

I understand Mary Martin had forty-nine shots of Novocain jabbed into her shoulders while she was playing Peter Pan and flying through the air "with the greatest of ease."

Suffer, but don't let anybody know it.

I quoted William Bernbach earlier in this book as saying that when they started Volkswagen ads they had so little money they had to make one ad do the work of ten. So they used, not funny ads, but concepts and copy tinged beautifully with humor. And, to repeat, they get big-store results for Ohrbach's with about one-thirtieth the money spent by New York's biggest department store.

Only the excessively well-heeled spenders can afford to be heavy-handed in advertising. Millions of dollars can accomplish almost anything. But who wants to use brute force to knock down a wall, when a relatively inexpensive stepladder will enable you to scale it?

If you want to win people, you must be as informal, human, and relaxed as people are. Somehow you must crack up your dignity and leave peepholes into your soul.

I repeat, the inability to smile, to "break it up," is costing American advertisers fortunes. Many of them are alienating people instead of attracting them.

Here's an analogy. Let's say that two products are identically the same (and product similarity is closer than you think in almost any line in which you are contemplating a purchase). Two salesmen can go out with almost identical prod-

ucts into the same territory, and one salesman can come back with ten times as many orders as the other. He doesn't do it with arguments, because each salesman has an almost identical list of arguments. He doesn't do it with funny stories.

He does it with a better personality. He is just "a pleasant guy to have come around to see you." He is no comedian, but he has a sense of humor. He is a more attractive human being. He is so easy-going that he does not create resistance.

Ralph Eckerstrom, director of advertising of Container Corporation of America, says: "In this day of similar technology, the only real advantage one company may have over its competitors is artistic creativity."

George Gribbin, chairman of Young & Rubicam, says: "Much advertising will rely on mood instead of overstated logic to develop distinctiveness for a brand."

Advertisers on the whole should relax. For advertising is, after all, a pretty easy proposition. It's almost a cinch. It's something like hitting a golf ball. It pays to know how, but you mustn't try to sock it too hard.

The only really bad advertisement I ever produced was one in which I forgot to put the name of the product.

↑ ↑ ↑

An Ad Man's Notes and Quotes

One way to get vulgarity out of advertising is to get humor into it.

✦ ✦

The one serious conviction that a man should have is that nothing should be taken too seriously.

—SAMUEL BUTLER

✦ ✦

Tommy Armour, seated under an umbrella at the teaching tee at Boca Raton, said, "I want to set them the example of educated languor." In advertising, as well as in golf, you can miss by pressing too hard. Controlled relaxation, or "educated languor," is necessary in both.

✦ ✦

One of the best pieces of advertising copy I've ever read is on a bronze tablet on the façade of The Second National Bank at Cumberland, Maryland. It reads: "The Old Big Strong Bank."

✦ ✦

Young Profession

Advertising suffers greatly because it is created by a new profession. It lacks the centuries of background which lie behind many other arts and businesses.

It is practiced largely by outsiders, without much training for it, or without even a modicum of cultivated interest in it.

Advertising today is a highly lucrative profession which, like the selling of insurance, real estate, or automobiles, is wide open to anybody with little or no preliminary schooling, discipline, or training—and often to men who have failed at many other things.

I do not mean to say that there are not many fine professional men among insurance, real estate, and automobile salesmen.

✦ ✦

The above may seem to conflict with the following, but I say not necessarily.

A man is sunk unless he retains the amateur in himself. You have got to have some of the enthusiasm, some of the eagerness of the amateur.

—RONALD COLEMAN

✦ ✦

I wonder sometimes if all the carefully planned research we promulgate is more valuable than the impressions we gain from our personal relationships. A half-hour with one's secretary, just talking about "what did *you* do yesterday?" may be just as revealing as a 37 per cent return to a survey among "working females in the New York metropolitan area."

197

The finest advertising copy our business has produced, I am sure, has come from people who have written from their sensitive, personal reactions to what other people feel and think. "Somewhere West of Laramie" was certainly no product of statistical research, but of a man who instinctively knew that an automobile is, to most people, an exciting possession.

As we enter a new year that offers its full challenge to creative advertising men and women I am willing to make this prediction: the year's best copy will come not from cold research, but from someone who loves people, devotes a lot of time to knowing them, and has a highly sensitive reaction to what they feel and want.—FRED DECKER, Publisher, *Printers' Ink*

⚹ ⚹

Public relations is the letter you don't write when you're mad and the nice letter you write the s.o.b. the next day after you're regained your sense of humor.

⚹ ⚹

Easy Goin'

It is no accident that we so often speak of grace as languid. One of the first lessons the movie directors learned was that the actors must move to a slow, steady tempo. Count off as a good screen actress moves about the screen and notice how long it takes her to remove or put on a wrap, to come through a door and close it behind her—yet every foot of film is costly. That's why home movies are jerky, often ridiculously so. We move too fast. A graceful woman, a well-poised man never hurries, at least, never gives you the impression of haste. It's the snatchers and jerkers who bump into the chairs and tip over the water glasses.—RUTH CHANDLER MOORE

⚹ ⚹

Anything that is unbelievable or silly lacks humor.

⚹ ⚹

Before long, the day of the shouter will be gone.
—GEORGE GRIBBIN, chairman of Young & Rubicam

⚹ ⚹

George Bernard Shaw believes style to be a by-product of sincerity.

⚹ ⚹

Humility: The sea, by lying low, receives all the waters of the world.—CHINESE PROVERB

⚹ ⚹

He who laughs lasts.—STEVE PRICE

⚹ ⚹

Don't take your advertising so seriously that nobody else will.

⚹ ⚹

The lighter the touch, sometimes the heavier the wallop.

⚹ ⚹

⚹ ⚹

Gaiety

A Southern lady once observed to me that gaiety is one of the surest marks of the aristocrat, and it is one of the unwritten laws of French politeness that a long face is a breach of manners. The truth of this does not need much pondering. To put a laughing face on the worst is not merely the top of courage, but it shows a well-bred consideration of our neighbors. Because things have gone wrong with us is no reason for pouring gloom on another's sunshine. Gaiety, in short, is one of the most important of our social duties, and one of the most attractive things about the soldier is the manner in which he laughs over the grimmest of all jobs.—RICHARD LE GALLIENNE

Shrewd

When will some shrewd manager be shrewd enough to perceive that in a world full of dull shrieking, the still small voice, the boast foregone, the falsehood dispensed with, the absurdity renounced, the fact understated, or stated with demurely delicate precision, have power to pique and almost to startle? Imagine a tube station wall on which half the plays running were puffed in the insipidly bawling old way and the other half were sized up, with a fastidious nicety and containment, for just what they were worth—a weak third act admitted, and comparison with real greatness disclaimed—but still quite an amusing piece on the whole, as pieces go now. With what a glow of respectful liking one's heart would warm to the play thus announced!—C. E. MONTAGUE, *A Writer's Notes on His Trade*

✔ ✔

Oh God, give me young men with brains enough to make fools of themselves.—ANONYMOUS

✔ ✔

Once in a while we have this happen in advertising: it tells a lie about a product which its sponsor realizes it had better hurry and live up to.

✔ ✔

Advertising Has Its Limits

I believe that a great deal of false and misleading copy comes about and is condoned chiefly because of the mistaken notion that copy can itself either make or close the sale. The whole cult of so-called "hard sell," in my opinion, is based on this wholly mistaken assumption.

Those who write advertising copy and those who approve it—and, above all, those who pay for its public dissemination—should, I believe, constantly bear in mind that if advertising copy is to be at all effective in contributing to the eventual sale, it should not venture beyond its limited province of informing favorably; of inciting curiosity; of building

belief; of creating understanding; of developing the urge to investigate and see for oneself.

—WALTER WEIR

✔ ✔

Subject: You

But I rise to inquire whether the subject of a really *good* advertisement is the product it advertises—or the reader? Whether a man can't learn what will help him to put over Moffett's Marmalade as well on the car going home from work at night, or by reading the Old Testament, and the New, or by attending Hamlet, or otherwise by rubbing up against life and people, as by visiting the Moffett plant and inspecting the vats?—MONCRIEFF HAMILTON SPEAR

✔ ✔

Natural

I will only say a word as to what you ask about style in writing. The best style that a man can hope for is a free, unconscious expression of his own spontaneity, not an echo of someone else. Therefore, although one can learn by reading, the help is only indirect. No one could imitate Burke with success, and speaking from old recollection, one wouldn't want to imitate Pater. Artificiality may be natural to him, but an artificial following of artificiality would be fatal. To illustrate what I mean, when you read Tennyson you feel that he has been carefully reaching for the exquisite. When you read Shakespeare you feel as if the splendid speech came without effort, because that was the way he wanted to talk. Stevenson searches for a happy word. Kipling rips an unusual word out of the bowels of the dictionary, and in his lips it sounds as natural as slang.

—OLIVER WENDELL HOLMES

✔ ✔

Nothing astonishes men so much as common sense and plain-dealing.—RALPH WALDO EMERSON

✔ ✔

✔ ✔

There is nobody so lacking in a sense of humor as a man in a hurry.

Our species is the only creative species, and it has the only one creative instrument—the individual mind and spirit of a man. Nothing was ever created by two men. There are no good collaborations, whether in music, art, poetry, mathematics, philosophy. Once the miracle of creation has taken place, the group can build and extend it, but the group never invents anything. The preciousness lies in the lonely mind of a man.—JOHN STEINBECK, in *East of Eden*

✦ ✦

Work is a form of nervousness.

✦ ✦

I'm utterly delighted with a quotation from Edwin H. Land, president of Polaroid Land Cameras, in an article in *Life:* "Every creative act is a sudden cessation of stupidity."

✦ ✦

Four Sore Fingers

One night on the subway I looked at five display cards in the end of the car. Four of them didn't expect to be seen, so their designers had placed a dominant rectangle in each at a certain acute angle. These cards were all trying so hard to be "different" that they succeeded only in being the same. The fifth card looked as if it expected itself to be read. It was printed in plain type in horizontal lines—a very unprofessional looking card among a company of overprofessional cards. It stood out like a well thumb alongside four sore fingers.

When everybody else is zigzag, I think it is smart to be straight. When everybody else is serious, I think it is wise to be a little light. When everybody else is having a contest, I think it is a relief to have no contest. When everybody else is shouting, I think it is wise to speak quietly. When everybody else is setting type cockeyed, I'll set mine as if I expected it to be read.

When everybody else is excited and frantic, I think it is much more attention-getting to be calm.

✦ ✦

Nobody responds to a salesman who is ridiculous; people pull away from pomposity; nobody buys from a braggart; and innocuous salesmen get only one response—indifference.

And yet advertising is full of ridiculous ideas (*"Don't let romance fade—fade—fade away"*) and pompous ideas (*"They said it couldn't be done"*) and braggart ideas (*"The greatest name in rubber"*) and innocuous ideas (*"Summertime is sandwich time."*)—ROBERT PRITIKIN, of Fletcher Richards, Calkins & Holden, Inc.

✦ ✦

British historian Arnold Toynbee believes that the stimulation of personal consumption through advertising is unchristian ("I cannot think of any circumstance in which advertising would not be an evil"), and last year advanced the extravagant notion: "The destiny of our Western civilization turns on the issue of our struggle with all that Madison Avenue stands for more than it turns on the issue of our struggle with Communism."

Says William Bernbach: "Mr. Toynbee's real hate is not advertising. It is the economy of abundance."

Without advertising, your Ford might cost you $500 more, and your favorite can of peas might be $1.50.

✦ ✦

Many of advertising's most virulent critics overstate the influence of advertising on consumers and understate the ability of the consumer to take care of himself.—NEIL H. BORDEN, Professor of Advertising

✦ ✦

In the complicated situations of life, we have to solve many problems and make many decisions by intuition. Reason alone is too slow and too difficult. —IRVING LANGMUIR, Nobel Prize winner in chemistry

✦ ✦

Cheerfulness is the atmosphere in which all things thrive.—JEAN PAUL RICHTER

✦ ✦

THE END

200